A DASH OF
MUSTARD

A DASH OF MUSTARD

Mustard in the Kitchen & on the Table:
»><« *Recipes & Traditions* **»><«**

KATY HOLDER AND JANE NEWDICK
WITH EXTRA MATERIAL BY IAN WISNIEWSKI

Reader's Digest

PUBLISHED BY THE READER'S DIGEST ASSOCIATION LIMITED
LONDON • NEW YORK • SYDNEY • CAPE TOWN • MONTREAL

A READER'S DIGEST BOOK

Published by The Reader's Digest Association Limited
Berkeley Square House
Berkeley Square
London W1X 6AB

ISBN 0-276-42187-6

This book was designed and produced by
Quarto Publishing Plc
The Old Brewery
6 Blundell Street
London N7 9BH

Art Director: Moira Clinch
Design: Design Revolution
Senior Art Editor: Liz Brown
Copy Editors: Jackie Matthews and Fiona Hunter
Home Economist: Katy Holder
Picture Researcher: Susannah Jayes
Picture Manager: Giulia Hetherington
Senior Editor: Sian Parkhouse
Editorial Director: Mark Dartford
Photographer: Philip Wilkins
Illustrator: Rodney Shackell

Typeset in Great Britain by Central Southern Typesetters, Eastbourne
Manufactured in Hong Kong by Regent Publishing Services Ltd
Printed in China by Leefung-Asco Printers Ltd

Contents

>><<

INTRODUCTION

MUSTARD IS A SIMPLE, EVERYDAY KIND OF SPICE, STRONG BUT HOMELY. IT HAS ALWAYS HAD AN IMPORTANT BUT UNDERSTATED ROLE IN THE KITCHEN, AND AT ONE TIME THE SICKROOM TOO, THOUGH IT WAS SOMETIMES OVERLOOKED IN FAVOUR OF RARER AND MORE EXOTIC SPICES. A REAL STALWART IN MANY CUISINES, MUSTARD ADDS HEAT AND PUNGENCY, SUBTLE FLAVOUR AND BRILLIANT COLOUR TO PLAIN OR ELABORATE MEALS.

Perhaps because it has always been an easy plant to cultivate and is more or less ubiquitously grown throughout the world, the small creamy yellow or brown seeds of mustard have often been taken for granted as an ingredient and spice. Throughout its long history, mustard is a flavouring which has sometimes been used carelessly or indis-criminately in the kitchen, gaining a reputation for heat with no subtlety which is really very unfair. Mustard deserves better than this, as we set out to prove here through history, anecdote, myth and inspiration.

The seeds of the mustard plant have been used as a spice, a condiment and a medicine for as long as it is possible to trace, with evidence that early civilizations living along the Indus valley around 2,300 BC – and even earlier – seasoned their meat with it.

Mustard seed comes from a small annual plant of the *cruciferae* family and there are three important types: white, black and brown. The colours refer to the colour of the ripened seed, not the flowers, which are bright yellow. White mustard (*brassica alba*) is naturalised throughout northern Europe and North America, while black mustard (*brassica nigra*) is native to southern Europe and temperate western Asia. Brown mustard (*brassica juncea*) is native to India. The mustards are part of a vast plant family which includes all the cabbages and broccolis, radish and watercress as well as

A field of mustard in full bloom is a memorable sight on a sunny day, with the vivid yellow of the flowers contrasting with a deep blue sky.

non-edible varieties such as wallflowers. None of these cruciferous plants is poisonous and all have antiscorbutic properties (meaning that they purify the blood). The seeds have to be harvested when they are completely ripe, but before they have burst from their little pea-shaped pods. Because black mustard seeds are hard to harvest – and is a process best done painstakingly by hand harvesting, brown mustard has now taken over from the black variety in commercial production as it can be harvested economically on a large scale, using machines.

Mustard seeds when crushed produce an oil which is fierce and pungent. Used externally, this oil first irritates then partially anaesthetises the sensory nerves and so it has been used for centuries to relieve the symptoms of rheumatism, gout and arthritis as well as colds and fever. Taken internally in large quantities, mustard oil is a powerful emetic, but used in smaller doses it has the effect of a digestive and diuretic, and also a stimulant. Other remedies incorporating mustard include chewing the seeds to relieve toothache and gargling for a sore throat with an infusion of

mustard and warm wine. Mustard footbaths were a popular everyday treatment until quite recently, and mustard baths for the whole body have been in and out of fashion over the centuries. Poultices have definitely gone out of vogue, but these messy "bandages" were regularly prescribed for all manner of ailments at one time, and often included mustard in their list of ingredients.

EARLY USES

In medieval times mustard was often used in cooking as a palliative to make old or badly preserved meat and dried fish edible by masking strong or rancid flavours. Its name in English suggests how it was used, as *must* is Anglo-Saxon for unfermented grape juice, with which it was commonly mixed, and *ardens* means hot or fiery. The seeds were used whole or roughly crushed in early times, as the dry mustard powder with which we are all familiar was not invented until late in the spice's history.

Every culture and country tends to have their mustard specialities and often towns or areas in each country where mustard production and processing is centred. French mustard, for example, is synonymous with the name Dijon – the town where the highly important French mustard industry is based. The French version is flavourful and sometimes grainy and mixed with wine vinegars, while the Americans love a sweet variety squeezed straight from a plastic bottle onto hot dogs and burgers. Because of its versatility and availability, mustard is often used in many cuisines as just one of many varied flavourings in a dish but it also has specific uses. It is often used simply to add heat, which it does in many cases in Indian and Japanese food and is also commonly used as an ingredient for pickling. At one time it was a

*B*rassica sinapsis, *or
wild mustard, is also
called charlock. A field
that seems to be clear of
this weed can be ploughed
up after several years and
quickly become a complete
mass of yellow flowers.*

8

cheaper way of adding ferocious heat than costly black pepper and of course it was around before the arrival of chillies in Europe. It can also be used to give its own subtle flavour: for example, in recipes for mustard sauces which are often designed to be used with specific foods like oily fish. Think of mackerel with mustard sauce, or the Italian *mostarde e frutta candita* served with boiled meats. But it is often in its less obvious uses as catalyst and enhancer to other ingredients that mustard really shines. What mayonnaise or vinaigrette dressing would be worth eating without a little mustard to help the emulsion along, and how much less piquant would many cheese dishes be without a pinch of the magical paste or powder?

Dijon, the French mustard city

It was the Romans who first introduced mustard to France (or Gaul, as it then was) and the French took to it wholeheartedly. The centre of the French mustard industry has always been Dijon in Burgundy, the wine and vinegar producing area. By the fourteenth century the town's mustard makers had adopted their own commercial trademark from the motto of the Duke Philip the Bold: "Moult me Tarde", or "I ardently desire". Some people claim this was abbreviated into "moustarde" – hence the French name for the condiment. The Dijon style of mustard was a blend of mustard seed and grape must, although variations added honey, oil, and vinegar.

By the end of the fifteenth century, mustard was losing ground to other spices and it remained in decline until the early eighteenth century, when a certain Monsieur Jean Naigeon invented a new recipe using verjuice instead of vinegar. The wine growers of Burgundy were happy to supply as much verjuice as was needed. It was a great success, and this period saw the beginnings of many of the great family companies with such well-known names as Maille and Grey Poupon. Dijon is still as important as ever to the French mustard industry and home to large companies such as SEGMA Liebeg Maille which includes Maille, Grey Poupon and Amora.

The winegrowers of Burgundy and the mustard makers of Dijon worked together to give the region a reputation for its mustard that endures today.

9

A fine collection of old ceramic mustard pots on display in Dijon, France.

THE PLANT

USUALLY PLANTED BETWEEN LATE FEBRUARY AND EARLY APRIL THROUGHOUT THE TEMPERATE WORLD, MUSTARD PLANTS NEED NO SPECIAL CARE TO FLOURISH. THEIR FAMILIAR BRIGHT YELLOW FLOWERS PROVIDE SPLASHES OF COLOUR IN THE LANDSCAPE.

Brown mustard.
Brassica juncea
The plant has vigorous and plentiful leaves, while the flower stems are smaller with more delicate and widely spaced flowers.

Mustard belongs to the *cruciferae* group of plants, a name which stems from the characteristic four petals of the flower which form the shape of a cross. All mustard varieties are annuals and easily grown from seed. The seed pods are harvested in the summer and early autumn when ripe, but before they burst, scattering the seeds.

Three types of mustard plant are grown. These are *brassica nigra* (black mustard), *brassic juncea* (brown mustard), and *brassica alba*, sometimes called *brassica hirta* or *sinapis alba* (white mustard). These names, stemming from the colour of the seeds, provide a ready colour coding. Black mustard seeds, with their dark rusty colour, are the smallest of the three types, though the plant itself towers over the others, reaching a height of three metres or more.

Originally a native of southern Europe, the Middle East and Western Asia, black mustard used to be cultivated throughout Europe, and, since it yields the most flavour of all, was many producers' first choice. However, what it offers in terms of flavour it exacts in production. It can grow to be very tall and needs rich soil to thrive and is brittle, which means the seeds can be released too easily. This makes commercial mechanical harvesting very difficult. So black mustard has become the preserve of peasant farmers who can harvest by hand in places such

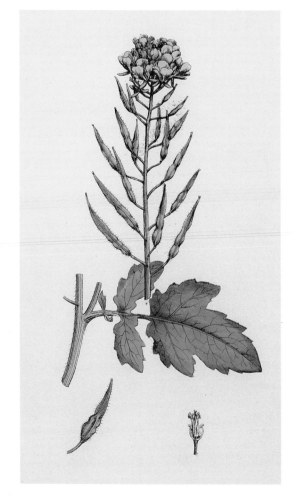

White mustard.
Brassica alba
The bright yellow flowers slowly open up the length of the stem and the pods set seed in sequence. The seed pods are larger than those of the black mustard plant, hold about three seeds and are covered in hairs.

as Sicily, Ethiopia, the CIS and India.

Brown mustard production has stepped in to take the place of black as it can be harvested mechanically. The plants are shorter, growing up to about one metre – with paler yellow flowers than black but the dark, reddish-brown seeds are larger than black ones, although less pungent. It is native to Africa, India, China and Pakistan.

White mustard, which is indigenous to the Mediterranean and central Europe, is now grown in most temperate climates worldwide, including the USA, Canada and Great Britain. As a plant it grows to about 80 centimetres and flourishes in heavy or sandy loam. The seeds of white mustard are the largest of the three kinds, but have the mildest flavour.

Black mustard.
Brassica nigra
The leaves are large and coarse but the seed pods are smooth and small and held close to the stems. The branching flower stems have small, narrow leaves, tapering to a point at each end.

A large field of mustard being cut with a horse-drawn reaper between the world wars in Britain. The cut plants have been gathered into small bundles and stood in stooks.

11

A Canadian field of white mustard in full flower. Canada has become one of the largest growers of mustard seed, particularly since the Second World War, and is the world's largest exporter of the crop.

MUSTARD IN THE KITCHEN

ALTHOUGH WE THINK FIRST OF THE SEEDS WHEN IT COMES TO THE CULINARY USES OF MUSTARD, ALMOST ALL PARTS OF THE PLANT CAN BE USED IN COOKING.

As a cooking ingredient, mustard has a more complex role than most simple spices. True, a pinch can be added to the cheese dish, for example, to add a little heat and a subtle flavour, but mustard is often used in a more considered way – as a crucial part of a recipe, not just a flavouring afterthought. It also has an important part to play as a thickener and, in the case of oil-based sauces or dressings, as an aid to emulsification. Like many other spices, it has a definite affinity with certain foods – think of mustard and herrings, or mustard and pork. This may have as much to do with the mustard acting as a digestive for these oily foods as it does to a happy marriage of two flavours. But there are other cases, where mustard and certain other ingredients – like tomatoes, or green beans – simply combine beautifully, and it is really quite hard to say why they do so.

People have relished spicy heat in foods for centuries, with mustard reigning supreme as the provider of this stimulation until peppercorns became widely exported. Mustard adds more than heat, however, it is its subtle flavour more than the fierceness which has really been explored in many classic dishes and combinations of food. In fact, cooking heat will reduce the pungency of mustard, leaving only the flavour; so if heat is required, mustard should be added near the end of the cooking time and the dish should then be simmered gently, for as short a time as possible.

To make up mustard from powder to serve as a simple condiment with food, only cold water should ever be used – a point many people forget. The reason is this: on adding cold water to ground mustard seeds, a chemical reaction occurs between the enzyme myrosin and the glucosides sinigrin in black mustard seed, or sinalbin in white mustard seed. The water acts as a catalyst, allowing the myrosin to ferment the sinigrin producing the essential oil of mustard (allyl isothiocyanate), potassium salt and sugar, which gives it a sharp taste and strong smell. The myrosin acts on the sinalbin to make sulpho-cyanate of acrinyl, sulphate or

sinapine and sugar milder in taste and less aromatic. If hot water is used instead, the chemical reaction goes awry, leaving heat but also a bitterness and a lack of flavour. All this science in the kitchen is therefore very important, but all you need to know is that to make the strong and distinctive taste of English mustard, *cold* water is essential. Always let mustard stand after mixing for ten minutes before eating it.

FLAVOURS OF THE ORIENT

Whole mustard seeds can be coarsely ground and added to foods or they can be used complete, in recipes such as pickled vegetables. Alternatively, they can be crushed with other spices for more complex seasonings to make eastern-inspired dishes, or toasted quickly until they start popping and added as a flavouring to some Indian dishes. Mustard oil is mainly used for cooking, mostly in certain Eastern recipes. White mustard leaves are eaten raw when young as salads, and when older can be cooked very briefly, as in a Chinese stir fry. Mustard powder is used to make mustard paste, usually mixed with water, and eaten as a relish with many foods, especially roast meats, served hot or cold, sautéed steaks, grilled fish and many other, mainly protein-rich, foods. This is powerful stuff, generally eaten only in very small quantities. A pinch or two of dry mustard is useful when making mayonnaise or vinaigrette dressings.

A coarse-grain mustard, in which the seeds have been only lightly crushed, adds texture as well as flavour to a dish.

14

The younger leaves of the mustard plant have a distinctive taste which holds its own against strong dressings.

Mustard, with its many uses, would have been relied upon in the nineteenth-century kitchen as much as other staples, such as flour and eggs.

The Story of Mustard

Originally a weed growing unnoticed amongst cereal crops, mustard has been cultivated for its usefulness for at least 5,000 years. History is littered with references to it and recipes for cooking with it.

Fish formed a regular part of the Roman diet, as this fishing scene from a third-century BC Sicilian mosaic indicates. Recipes show that mustard was used frequently in a number of fish dishes.

In the early days, mustard leaves were eaten as a food as often as the seeds were used for flavouring. (The leaves are still eaten today, especially in Asian countries.) In the second century AD, the Roman emperor Diocletian classified mustard as a food, not a condiment, perhaps for this reason. Nor is mustard described in the Bible as a condiment, but it is mentioned in the parable of the mustard seed (Mark 4), where Jesus compares the kingdom of God to a grain of mustard "which when it is sown in the earth, is less than all the seeds that be in the earth. But when it is sown, it groweth up, and becometh greater than all herbs, and shooteth out great branches; so that the fowls of the air may lodge under the shadow of it".

The earliest known cultivation and use of mustard was in India and China around 3000 BC, where it was used to enliven a dull and monotonous diet of wheat and barley and some meats, cooked in sesame oil. By the time ancient Greek civilization was thriving, mustard was a common ingredient. It was often eaten in small handfuls and chewed with meat, producing a nutty flavour which also helped to mask less than perfect ingredients. The ancient Egyptians had also eaten mustard in this way.

The Greeks knew that mustard aided the digestion and had antiseptic properties: they used it in many different medicines and remedies, as well as in the kitchen. Both the ancient Greeks and the Romans had names for mustard which later came to inspire botanists to give the plant its scientific Latin name *sinapsis*.

From seed to paste

It was the Romans who began to realize the full potential of mustard by turning it into a paste with the addition of grape must (unfermented grape juice), vinegar, oil and honey. Mustard was also used as a kind of pickling spice and preservative for meats, again often mixed with honey, salt and vinegar. Crushed mustard seeds were sprinkled on all manner of dishes. The Romans had a passion for many different kinds of strongly flavoured sauces, several of which included mustard. To our modern tastes they sound disgusting, relying as they did on rotted

Pliny the Elder (AD 33-79) outlined the medicinal uses of mustard in his Natural History, *which remained a key scientific work until the Renaissance.*

16

fish entrails and similar ingredients. *Liquamen* or *garum* was a salty fermented fish sauce, not unlike those found in Thailand, Vietnam and Cambodia today. *Muria* was another, made with mustard and the brine drained from preserved tunafish.

Mustard was not universally popular in Rome, however – Plautus declared that "man fed on mustard could not be more sour and insensate". In his text written in the third century BC, he actually condemned it as a "frightful poison". Apicius, the gourmand who lived through the reigns of Emperors Augustus and Tiberius, had no such qualms about any foods – he ate everything, with great enjoyment and in huge quantities. Apicius's party-throwing was renowned. When he had squandered all his money on feasts and fabulous meals, he decided life would no longer be worth living. He ordered one last banquet to end all banquets, included in which was one poisoned dish for him to eat and take his own life. He left behind the most comprehensive book on Roman cookery we have, called *De Re Coquinaria* (On Cookery).

The Byzantines added mustard to their food by way of sauces. They had several varieties, all of which relied on the seed as their crucial

≫≫⫷⫷

Catholic Tastes

His Holiness Pope John XXII reigned in Avignon from 1316 to 1334. He created the post of "grand moutardier du Pape" for his nephew, and was accused of nepotism for his pains.

≫⫷

One for the Pot

King Louis XI of France (1423–83) carried his own personal pot of mustard, made for him by a Dijon mustard maker. He had a disconcerting habit of arriving unannounced to eat with his Parisian subjects, producing the mustard pot at each meal.

flavouring. An early type of vinaigrette was popular, eaten with many sorts of foods and liberally spiced with mustard. Another favourite was a sauce made from mustard and oxymel (a drink flavoured with vinegar and honey).

THE POPE'S MUSTARD MAKER

The Romans are credited with bringing mustard to Gaul. There it was quickly taken up and successfully grown over the centuries, especially by the monks of St Germain des Près in Paris and other holy orders, who, during the tenth century and afterwards, became re-nowned for their skill in mustard making. It was a skill not limited to Paris by any means – by the thirteenth century the Provost of Paris had also granted the vinegar makers of Dijon the right to make mustard, and the latter city was on the way to becoming the French capital of the condiment.

There is a saying in France that: "*Il se prend pour le moutardier du pape*" or "he thinks himself the Pope's mustard maker." It is applied to people who are vain, arrogant and self-important. There are two versions of how the saying came about, the first one dating back to the time of Pope Clement VI. A member of the Medici family, Clement adored mustard and ate

17

Charles VI of France had a weakness for mustard in all his food, especially a peasant dish consisting of herb-coated chicken with a mustard sauce. His personal cook was the famous Taillevent, who began his career as a kitchen porter in the early fourteenth century.

CHARLES·VI·ROY·DE·FRANCE

it at every meal. Streams of people attempted to curry favour with the Pope by making delicious mustards for him. If there was one he really liked, the fortunate mustard maker would then receive many favours from the Pope. Those who were jealous would call the successful person "the Pope's mustard maker", particularly if they were prone to brag about their new honours. The second story relates how Pope John XXII (1316–34) had a ne'er-do-well nephew who was not even clever enough to become a cardinal (in those days an appointment often granted as a favour, unless you were

particularly stupid). The Pope therefore created a job for his nephew entitled "grand moutardier du pape" and ever afterwards this expression has denoted someone who is stupid and conceited.

Mustard was a spice used in every French household, rich and poor. There is a story about King Charles VI who, during one of his campaigns against the English, found himself in the besieged town of Sainte-Menehoud. Here he called upon the hospitality of an ordinary peasant, who cooked him a dish of chicken grilled with herbs and a breadcrumb coating, served with a mustard sauce. The king was delighted with this meal and from then on this special dish was recreated for him wherever he wanted it by his chef Taillevent. The king was so pleased with this chef that he was speedily elevated from kitchen porter to master of the king's kitchen. Taillevent went on to write what is now one of the oldest and most celebrated French cookery books, which gives a fascinating insight into the medieval world of food and includes recipes for such oddities as swan, heron and peacock.

The all-purpose spice

In Britain, mustard was used as frequently in cooking as it was in France, being a very cheap spice and also native grown. Cultivated white mustard was probably a Roman introduction, judging by the seeds that have been found on old Roman sites such as Silchester. By the early medieval period it had become a useful ingredient to relieve the monotony of pottage and salted meat, and in later centuries it was used in even greater quantity and in more inspiring ways. One record from 1418 describes the household of Dame Alicia de Breyene buying mustard for less than a farthing a pound (500 g). In one year, 84 pounds of it were eaten. We do not know how large her household was,

In the Middle Ages, poultry and meat joints would have been fatty and often tough. Slow cooking over a spit or in a large pot helped to counteract these drawbacks, as did the judicious addition of mustard.

but over one and a half pounds of mustard a week is a very large amount of spice! Mustard was usually made at home by crushing the seeds in a small quern, or mill, and then mixing them with water or vinegar, but it could also be bought from professional sauce makers or "mustarders". Mustard was essential eating with salt fish, particularly herrings and stockfish (dried and salted cod and similar fish). Another dish which always required mustard was brawn. Made from the head and fatty foreparts of a pig or boar, it invariably preceded other meats and fish at large meals. Popular from the thirteenth century until at least the seventeenth century, it featured in the feast to celebrate Neville's enthronement as Archbishop of Canterbury in 1467. The meal began with brawn and mustard served with malmsey (a sweet wine).

By the sixteenth century, the mustarders and sauce-makers had been joined by millers, who ground the mustard seed and sold it as a dry powder or a paste. One town in particular now became famous for its mustard production. Tewkesbury in Gloucestershire was a thriving wool town with plenty of other industry, too, such as tanning and leatherworking. Mustard making was chiefly a cottage industry carried out by the women of the town, who probably collected their own mustard seed from the

An illustration of King Charles VI's chef, Taillevent. He had great influence as a gastronome and cook until his death in 1395. Here he discusses fresh produce with a supplier of poultry.

nearby fields and ground it in iron mortars – not with iron pestles, but with cannon balls. This coarse flour was mixed with pease flour and cinnamon, then moistened with a mixture of honey and vinegar (which had been infused with fiery horseradish root) and stirred for at least an hour. This stirring was thought to improve the mustard's texture and keeping qualities. The resultant paste was formed into balls the size of hens' eggs and then dried. The balls kept well, so could be sent across country. To reconstitute them they were combined with water, vinegar, butter-milk, ale, cider – or indeed, whatever took your fancy. The horse-radish may have been the master stroke: Tewkesbury mustard became famous and Thomas Tusser, author of *Five Hundred Points of Good Husbandry*

The reputation of Tewkesbury mustard was confirmed in Shakespeare's Henry IV part 1, in which Falstaff says of Poins that his wit was as "thick as Tewkesbury mustard". Today, however, mustard production in the town has completely died out.

19

Dijon remains the mustard capital of France today, just as it was in the fourteenth century.

claimed in 1662, that "the best mustard is made in Tewkesbury. It is very wholesome in clearing the head." However, some people complained of the expense of this speciality. In 1639, one Peter Munday, being asked to pay three or four pence for a ball of the stuff, declared that he would prefer a farthing's worth of prepared mustard paste, which was "like the old dried thicke scurffe that sticks on the side of a mustard pot". The seventeenth century was the heyday of Tewkesbury mustard. Afterwards it seemed to have waned in popularity, with the wild plants continuing to grow around the town as a poignant reminder of its former glory.

MUSTARD MANIA

The next interesting development in mustard took place in the early eighteenth century in Durham, aided by a Mrs Clements. Mustard was still as popular as ever, and the spread of new tastes in food meant that there were always new ways to eat it. Moreover, many of the more exotic flavours and spices of the previous century were losing favour in place of simpler stalwarts such as mustard, herbs and pickles. Around 1720, Mrs Clements therefore devised a method of making very fine mustard flour without the oily mess usually produced when the

seed was ground too long. She put the seeds through several processes, rather like milling wheat, extracting any husk, and resulting in a smooth powder which was, apparently, mixed with cornflour and turmeric. By 1729 she had gone into full production and sold her powder throughout the country, delivering it herself to shops, markets and roadside stalls. Mrs Clements became a wealthy woman in the process and Durham continued to be a mustard centre until the end of the nineteenth century.

There were many other manufacturers who also benefited from the popularity of mustard. One of them was the famous Keen's from Garlic Hill in London, established in 1742 and believed to be the reason for the saying "as keen as mustard". By 1862, Keen's had merged with Messrs. Robinson and Bellville, who processed barley, and the new company held Royal warrants to supply King William IV, Queen Victoria and Emperor Napoleon III with their products. Keen's were conscious of the need for good advertising and used memorable images and wording such as "Never eat the national dish without the national condiment". The accompanying picture showed a monarch about to knight a large joint of beef with a page boy beside him holding the mustard. As Henry

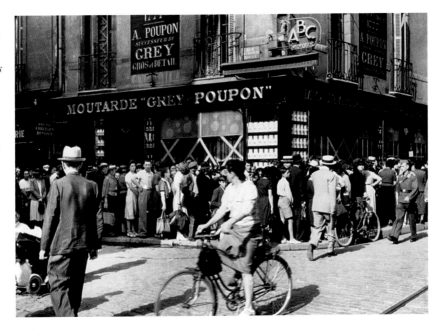

Grey Poupon mustard is one of the most famous in France, and the company jealously guards its reputation by keeping its mustard recipe locked in a safe. Maurice Grey revolutionized the industry in the nineteenth century by introducing new equipment which greatly speeded up production.

VII had inaugurated the idea of Sir Loin, it was hardly a new idea, but it sold plenty of mustard. Roast beef and mustard were by now seen as inseparable by the British public.

Colman's is another famous mustard name which remains well-known to this day. Established in Norwich, the Company eventually took over Keen's in 1903. They adopted their bull's head logo in 1850 and were granted a Royal warrant by Queen Victoria in 1866. The distinctive yellow packaging for their most famous product, mustard powder, is so well-known in Britain that Colman's simply *is* mustard to most people.

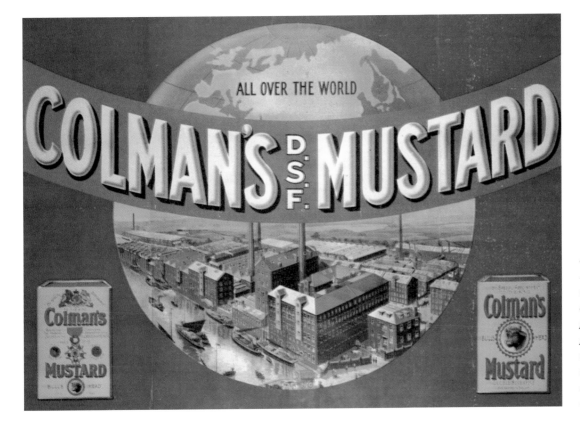

Colman's and mustard became synonymous in Britain at the beginning of this century. The company's best-known product has always been powdered mustard, but nowadays there are ready-mixed versions alongside the familiar yellow tins of powder.

HEALING MUSTARD

MOST OF US THINK OF MUSTARD AS AN ESSENTIAL REQUIREMENT IN ANY WELL-STOCKED MODERN KITCHEN, BUT WE TEND TO FORGET ITS LONG AND ILLUSTRIOUS MEDICINAL HISTORY.

Hippocrates, the early Greek physician and philosopher, was an avid exponent of preventative medicine though his views on treating illness were somewhat radical. "What cannot be cured by medicine must be cured by the knife; what cannot be cured by the knife must be cured by fire", he wrote. Mustard, especially in poultices, was an important part of his treatment to cure bronchitis, pneumonia and rheumatism.

It has been used for centuries as a medicinal ingredient in many different folk remedies. The important part of the plant has always been the seed, although mustard "greens", or leaves, have also been eaten for their health-giving benefits.

If mustard really did possess all the medicinal properties attributed to it, then a daily dose of it would surely help to make the world a much healthier place. Current medical opinion, however, does not rate mustard on the same level as those wonder foods, olive oil and garlic, but perhaps one day mustard will join their ranks.

The seeds contain a powerful, caustic oil, which has various properties. In the past, it was taken internally to stimulate the heart, respiratory system and digestion. For external use, mustard powder was a common addition to hot baths, poultices and skin plasters, used to relieve the symptoms of arthritis and rheumatism. It was also believed to help people who were suffering from colds or 'flu', or who were chilled by bad weather. A mustard foot-bath after a long, night-time ride on horseback was a favourite restorative for tired and shivering travellers. In medieval times, huge doses of mustard were taken after excessively large or spicy meals, and in these enormous quantities it would act as an emetic and diuretic. In smaller portions, mustard would work as a stabilizer and digestive for the over-burdened stomach. We still tend to eat mustard with rich and fatty foods today, as an aid to digestion. The little couplet "Sympathy without relief is like to mustard without beef" is, ironically, quite apt in this context.

THE MARVELLOUS CURE-ALL

The ancient Greeks were enthusiastic about the medicinal properties of mustard, believing that the very pungent black seeds, which are particularly sulphurous, were more health-giving than the brown or white ones. The

Aesculapius, son of Apollo, was credited with creating mustard, but its stimulating effect on the brain was in fact recognised before the time of the Greeks.

Greeks also ate the green leaves of the mustard plant, both raw and cooked, and Athenaeus mentions mustard alongside lettuce in his writings on salads. What we know today as mustard and cress is in fact unlikely to be mustard seedlings, but rather the seeds of the rape plant, though true mustard and cress was once grown from the seeds of white mustard and land cress. Athenaeus also writes about a special kind of mustard called Cyprus mustard (*napa kuprion*) which may be similar to the varieties in common use today. We do know that the Greeks cultivated mustard as a crop, rather than simply gathering it from the wild. In fact, mustard was such an important herb to the ancient Greeks that their god of medicine and

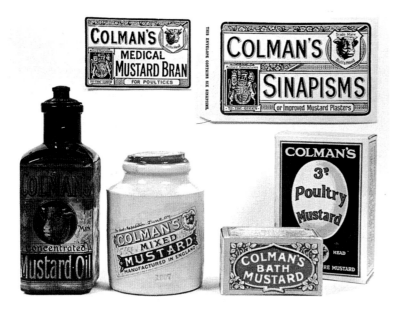

healing, Aesculapius, was credited with its creation.

"Mustard burns like fire" wrote the Roman Pliny in the 1st century AD. But he perceived it as a healing fire, citing mustard as a remedy for many ailments. He claimed that it was enough to simply place some mustard on a bite from even "the most venomous" snake to effect a cure and that eating the worst poisonous fungi was no problem if the mustard was consumed immediately afterwards. Pliny wrote several volumes of his *Natural History* on the medicinal qualities of plants – based, presumably, on his own observations, though we do not know how far his practical experimentation took him. He died neither from snake bites nor lethal mushrooms, but was a victim of the great eruption that obliterated Pompeii.

Both the Greeks and the Romans considered mustard to be an excellent stimulant, rousing not only the appetite but also the brain. They used the seeds both as an indigestion

The English name for a mustard plaster was a sinapism and in French it was sinapisme. Both words come from the Greek for white mustard Sinapsis alba. These packets contained mustard papers which would have had a similar effect as plasters.

treatment and as a laxative (in the latter case white mustard seeds were thought to be particularly effective). Chewing whole seeds with food was commonly practised as a means of flavouring meat, and also in cases of bad toothache, when the mustard oil would desensitize the inflamed gums. Other medical solutions stemmed from combining mustard seed with various liquids. One popular potion was made by infusing the seeds in heated wine or hot water. This was used as a gargle against sore throats, for treating bronchitis and congestion of the nose and chest, and even for the less threatening condition of hiccoughs.

THE MUSTARD POULTICE

One of the most traditional uses of mustard favoured by the Greeks and Romans was in the form of a poultice. This hot paste could be made from all manner of ingredients, mashed or ground up with a liquid of some kind to bind everything together. Designed to draw out heat and impurities from the body and to bring the blood to the surface of the skin, poultices have been used for many different ailments throughout the ages. Some were used specifically for wounds or skin infections, others for muscular aches and pains, or to relieve internal problems such as congestion in the lungs. A mustard poultice from Greek or Roman times might have been made from ground seeds mixed with hot water, spread onto muslin and wrapped like a

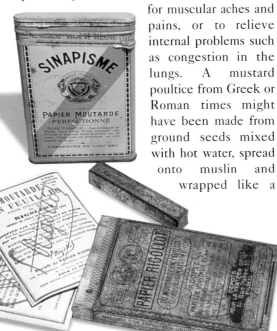

A range of Colman's mustards for many different uses – from mustard to eat, and taken on an Arctic expedition, to bran for making poultices. Mustard was used by poultry keepers to stop hens eating their own eggs which can commonly happen. A little mustard put into an egg shell soon puts them off the idea.

bandage round the affected part of the body. An alternative version was a paste made from ground seeds and vinegar, applied to the body and held in place. Both were likely to cause irritation to all but the toughest skin.

Hippocrates was a great advocate of the mustard poultice, generally preferring the vinegar paste recipe, which he used to treat bronchitis, rheumatism, pneumonia and neuralgia. Hippocrates was born into a medical family on the Greek island of Kos in the fifth century. He prescribed natural treatments, taken in conjunction with "preventative medicine", meaning a healthy diet and plenty of exercise. Though much of his time was taken up with medical matters, he also wrote several philosophical treatises, which were widely read.

The use of mustard to combat congestion and general respiratory problems was constantly being restated, especially during the Middle Ages, and its properties for aiding digestion were never disputed. John Gerard's *Herbal*, published in 1597, contains this example: "The seede of mustarde pounded with vinegar is an excellent sauce, good to be eaten with any grosse meates, either fish or flesh, because it doth help digestion, warmeth the stomach and provoketh appetitie". But according to John Evelyn, writing in 1699, mustard leaves were "of incomparable effect to quicken and revive the spirits, strengthening the memory, ex-pelling heaviness" and therefore provoking a rather different kind of appetite for life, relieving melancholia and depression.

CULPEPER'S LORE

The poultice was still a popular remedy for all types of illness in the 17th century, when the British herbalist and physician Nicholas Culpeper recommended putting a mustard poultice (made from ground mustard seed, breadcrumbs and vinegar) on the soles of the feet as an effective way of relieving fevers, sciatica and rheumatic pains. Vinegar was seen as another great cure-all, widely used as a medicine both internally and externally. The nursery rhyme "Jack and Jill" reminds us of its use as a dressing for bruises and wounds, wrapping poor unfortunate Jack's head "with vinegar and brown paper". Culpeper was an influential voice and remained so for many years. He first published his book The English

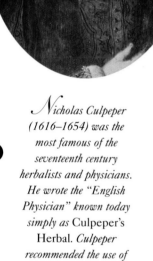

Nicholas Culpeper (1616–1654) was the most famous of the seventeenth century herbalists and physicians. He wrote the "English Physician" known today simply as Culpeper's Herbal. Culpeper recommended the use of mustard in poultices for fevers, sciatica and rheumatic pains.

Bruise Reliever

The ingredients might suggest this is an interesting sauce but in fact mustard seeds, onion and honey make an effective bruise and swelling reliever.

*2 parts mustard seed, ground with a pestle and mortar
1 part set honey
1 part finely chopped onion
Combine ingredients and apply to infected area, covering with a bandage or handkerchief.*

Gargle

A mustard gargle prepared with natural ingredients is an excellent way to fight off a sore throat.

*1 tbsp mustard seed, ground with a pestle and mortar
juice of half a lemon
1 tbsp salt
1 tbsp clear honey
1/2 pint boiling water
Combine ingredients and leave for about 15 minutes, covered.*

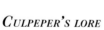

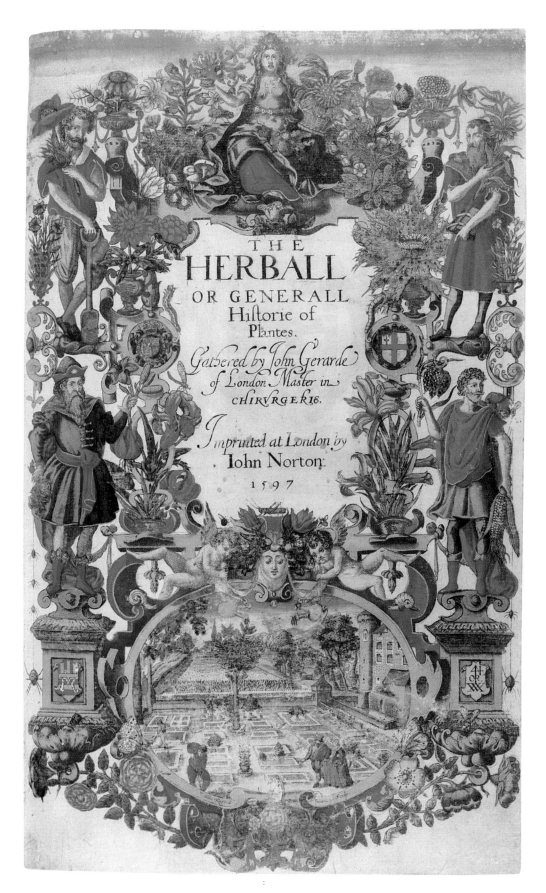

The frontispiece to The Herball *by John Gerarde published in 1597. He advocated the use of mustard as an aid to digestion and appetite.*

Physician Enlarged in 1653 and it was still being sold at the beginning of the nineteenth century. He advised that taking mustard was a sensible measure "whenever a stimulating medicine is wanted to act upon the nerves". By the eighteenth century a physician named Herberden was suggesting that mustard could help in asthma attacks, presumably because of the age-old belief that it was useful for respiratory diseases and ailments.

When mustard is made into a condiment, it should never be mixed with hot water, but medicinally it has long been used in hot baths. Ground black seeds were preferred for this purpose, and though ordinary kitchen mustard powder would have been perfectly adequate for bathroom use, nineteenth century manufacturers were quick to realize the potential of such a product. They were soon packaging bath mustard in special boxes, for humans and even for horses! It was sold as a marvellous pick-me-up and soother for rheumatic pain, stiff muscles, headaches and tired feet. Before clever packaging and marketing made mustard baths something special, ordinary people had quietly been using them for years. They were most commonly used to prevent colds and 'flu' in the days when people were convinced that colds could be caught by getting cold or wet. The great advantage of mustard over any other remedy was that it was always very cheap to buy and easy to obtain – most houses would have kept a large pot of it in the larder at all times.

Colman's managed to inject some style into the somewhat unappealing and messy idea of a mustard bath with its advertising campaign to promote the benefits of a long, hot soak. Just before the First World War, the firm was using an illustration of elegant figures waltzing around a ballroom, under the title "After the Dance – a Mustard Bath", suggesting that it would revive anyone who had danced the night away. Two or three tablespoons of the magic powder were claimed to be enough in a good deep hot bath. Presumably it did not stain the body yellow, but nevertheless it must have been quite a task for the poor person dealing with the endless cans of hot water to fill and empty the bath, in the days when mains plumbing and drainage were not commonplace. Another of mustard's uses was to clear a

muddy complexion by holding the head over a steaming bowl of mustard and boiling water, to open the skin's pores and remove blemishes. Mustard oil, however, was used in slightly different ways. Too powerful and irritating in its raw state, the oil had to be diluted in a carrier such as alcohol or camphor, when it could be used to treat chilblains, muscular pain or rheumatism. Mustard oil was even used as an alternative to wearing a wig or toupee – in theory, at least, the pungent oil can be rubbed into a bald or thinning scalp to stimulate the growth of hair.

❯❯❮❮

Mustard Bath

A good book, a gin and tonic and a long hot mustard bath provide perfect relaxation.

*4 tbsp mustard seeds,
ground with a pestle and mortar
a generous handful of bath sea salt
Sprinkle the mustard
and the salt together into the
bath tub as it fills.*

The footbath was the thing for anyone weary, cold or chilled from travelling and being outdoors in wintry weather. The clever use of colour in this advertisement says Colman's mustard.

Colman's produced a special mustard for baths, packaging it in an entirely different colour and style of box to make it seem as different as possible from the eating variety.

TO OPEN
Press here (breaking label) and raise lid.

BATH MUSTARD

MANUFACTURED BY
J. & J. COLMAN LTD.,
NORWICH & LONDON,
ENGLAND

COLMAN'S MUSTARD

"Returned from Klondyke"

A Mustard Atlas

Armchair travellers and cooks at home can choose from a worldwide range of different mustards. There are styles to suit every taste from Europe, America and Asia.

FRANCE

Mustard production is still centred around Dijon, but from this one area come many different varieties.

Dijon mustard: yellow, smooth and with a pronounced, pungent taste, made with finely ground black and brown seeds blended with liquid such as wine, verjuice (the juice from unripe grapes) or vinegar, plus spices and salt. Although it has been given an AOC (*Appelation Controlée*), with strict rules laid down about its ingredients, it can be made outside Dijon. Most French mustard, however, is still made in this region.

Bordeaux mustard: a mild flavour, using black and brown seeds, either ground fine or with some husk remaining. A darker colour than Dijon, and with a subtle sweet-sourness, it includes grape must (unfermented wine), vinegar and herbs such as tarragon.

Meaux mustard: medium hot and grainy, using partly crushed and partly ground black and brown seeds, blended with vinegar and spices. Made originally by the monks of Meaux in the early seventeenth century, the formula was given to the Pommery family in 1760. In 1826, Brilat-Savarin opined that: "the *only* mustard is Meaux mustard".

Florida mustard: mild, smooth and pale, made with champagne (or to be strictly technical, wines that are a by-product of champagne production and which do not qualify for the champagne name). When a champagne mustard was created in 1803, the maker Bourdin said that it "has a flavour, a bouquet, an aroma easier to rejoice at than describe".

Beaujolais mustard: has a claret colour and includes red ground seeds.

Champsac mustard: fragrant, smooth, dark, flavoured with fennel.

Moutarde a l'ancienne: mild flavour, coarsely ground seeds.

Fennel

BRITAIN

Traditionally renowned for its vivid yellow mustard powder. British mustard is composed of finely ground black, brown and white seeds with the husks removed, wheat flour and sugar, plus spices such as turmeric for colour. Powdered mustard is made up with cold water to a paste and allowed to stand for ten minutes or so while the flavour and heat develop.

Tarragon vinegar

Alternatively, a milk and cream combination, vinegar or beer can be used instead of water. Various prepared mustards are also produced, including local speciality ingredients such as ale, Scotch whisky, cider and English wine. One company has experimented with reviving the old tradition of flavouring horseradish sauce with mustard.

ITALY

Mostarda di frutta: fruit preserved in a mustard-flavoured syrup is "the" style of mustard in Italy. Commercial production is largely focused on *mostarda di Cremona*, while the other varieties are generally prepared domestically.

Mostarda di Cremona: uses whole fruits such as

Cinnamon

Peach

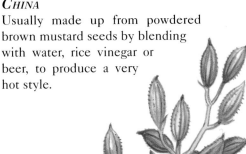

pears, cherries, apricots, peaches or figs, together with sliced fruits such as lemon, preserved in a syrup flavoured with mustard, white wine and honey.

Mostarda di Veneto: two versions are prepared, using either quinces or apples.

Mostarda alla Toscana (also known as *mostarda di Capri*): combines pears and apples simmered in vin santo, spiced with cinnamon, cloves and lemon zest, preserved in a syrup of grape must, infused with mustard seeds.

Mostardo di Piedmont: pumpkins, quinces, walnuts, toasted hazelnuts, pears and figs preserved in a mustard syrup based on must from Barbera grapes.

Mostarda di frutta piccante: the hottest variety, using various puréed fruits.

GERMANY

Dusseldorf mustard: usually mild, even slightly sweet and sour, though it can veer towards the full-bodied and pungent. Black mustard seeds are blended with vinegar, herbs and spices. Mid to dark brown colour.

Bavarian mustard: mild, coarse-grained.

Tafelsenf ("table mustard"): a mild, all-purpose style.

SWEDEN

Mild, sweet mustards prepared using vinegar, sugar and spices.

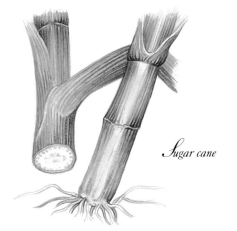

Sugar cane

AMERICA

American mustard: very mild, yellow paste made from white mustard seeds, vinegar or white wine, plus added spices such as turmeric and paprika.

American brown mustard: pale brown colour, with a subtle spiciness.

Creole mustard: brown colour, coarsely ground and sometimes mildly pungent.

Russian mustard: very hot and sweet.

CHINA

Usually made up from powdered brown mustard seeds by blending with water, rice vinegar or beer, to produce a very hot style.

Tumeric and paprika

29

Rice

JAPAN

Japanese mustard has neither the fragrance nor the subtlety of Western mustards. Available as a prepared paste or in powdered form, the latter is considered the superior version. Powder is made up with a little water in the base of a bowl, which is then inverted while the flavour develops, over about 15 minutes. It should be prepared just before serving, as the pungency soon fades. At its peak, though, this is strong stuff and little is needed.

First Choose Your Flavour

The wide range of flavoured mustards now available suits an ever wider range of uses, and, rather than choosing a flavoured mustard according to the dish you are serving, why not reverse the order, putting mustard first, and using its flavour as a starting point from which to choose the accompanying food? Here are some flavoured mustards, together with their suggested uses.

Mustard should be stored in a cool place, and once opened the container should be kept covered (to help prevent it from drying out) and refrigerated. No matter how old mustard grows, it will not develop bacteria or mould, though the flavour will fade.

Aniseed Mustard
Fish, dressings (ideal for carrot, beetroot, tomato or cucumber salad).

Basil

Real Ale Mustard
Stews, steaks, ham, sausages, robust cheeses, jacket potatoes.

Basil Mustard
White meat, on pizza, quiche or tart (beneath the topping), tomatoes.

Chilli Mustard
Spicy soups, stews, chilli con carne, sausages.

Chive Mustard
Salad dressings, in meat and fish sauces, potatoes.

Cider Vinegar Mustard
Roast pork, pork pies, ham, gammon, sausages, cheddar cheese.

Cognac Mustard
White meat, stews, salad dressings.

Coriander Mustard
Spicy soups, white meats (particularly pork), rice salads.

Chillies

Horseradish

Dill Mustard
Cured or smoked fish (gravadlax of course), shellfish, salad dressings, potatoes.

Garlic Mustard
Various meat (especially steak, barbecued sausages, poultry stuffings), Scotch eggs, vinaigrette, mayonnaise, vegetable purées.

Ginger Mustard
Herrings, chicken, turkey, veal, pork, oriental dishes, sauces, dressings.

Spiced Honey Mustard
Game, gammon, sweet-cured ham, smoked meats, cheese.

Ginger

Horseradish Mustard
Roast beef and Yorkshire, cold and boiled beef, fish sauces, baked potato dishes, beetroot salad.

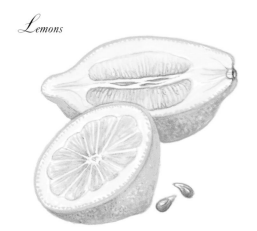

Lemons

LEMON MUSTARD
Roast chicken, veal, salad dressings, fish sauces, sautéed courgettes.

MINT MUSTARD
Lamb, especially leg, meatballs, salads, potato dishes, apple sauce.

BLACK OLIVE MUSTARD
Barbecued meat, pissaladiere, dressings (ideal for tomatoes).

ORANGE MUSTARD
Cold meat such as chicken, pork and duck, salad dressings.

Peanuts

PEANUT MUSTARD
Oriental dishes, chicken, salad dressings, sandwiches.

GREEN PEPPERCORN MUSTARD
Various meat (especially steak), meat fondues, vinaigrette, deglazing, sautéed mushrooms, savoury pancake batter.

PINK PEPPERCORN MUSTARD
Various meat, especially grilled, vegetable soups.

HERBS OF PROVENCE MUSTARD
Various meat, especially grilled, vegetable soups.

ROQUEFORT CHEESE MUSTARD
White meat (especially roast chicken), salad dressings.

SCOTCH WHISKY MUSTARD
Cold meat, game dishes, full-flavoured cheeses, meat sauces.

TARRAGON MUSTARD
White meat (ideal for roast chicken and chicken salad), dressings (especially tomato salad), soups.

VIOLET MUSTARD
Salad dressings, sauces, charcuterie.

Tarragon

31

Violets

Mustard around the World

MUSTARD HAS LONG BEEN A WORLDWIDE INGREDIENT, AND MANY COUNTRIES HAVE THEIR OWN INDIGENOUS VARIETIES, LEADING TO A REPERTOIRE OF MUSTARD CUISINE.

A range of British Victorian main course dishes, such as sirloin of beef and leg of mutton, which without doubt would have been served with mustard for anyone who wished it.

Some of these dishes have stood the test of time, while others are currently out of fashion, but as mustard has been around for so long, some dishes which are all but forgotten now may well be rediscovered in the future. The cuisines of India, Asia, the Mediterranean, the Balkan states, the Caribbean, the USA, Northern Europe and Africa all make use of mustard in some form or other.

France, often thought of as the true home of mustard (it still produces over half the world's output of made mustard) has a large repertoire of ways to use it, spanning classic sauces and dressings such as mayonnaise, vinaigrette and the garlicky *aoli* to *ragouts* and *daubes*. French dressing is generally made with Dijon mustard, but a dash of the champagne-flavoured version makes a special alternative. It is also good in sauces and for fish or chicken, and most spicy dishes. Sauces for vegetables and grilled meats are superbly partnered by Meaux or white wine mustard.

Amongst France's signature dishes are *lapin à la moutarde* (rabbit baked with mustard and served with a mustard sauce) and a variation on this theme of *poulet moutarde Dijonnaise*

Cured salmon is a Swedish speciality, invariably served with a mustardy sauce.

(chicken with a wine, cream, cheese and mustard sauce finished with breadcrumbs).

PERFECT PARTNERS
Northern Europe has its vast array of smoked, cured, pickled and salted meats, which are often served with mustard of some kind. Germany has sausage specialities – probably up to 1,000 different kinds – which are tailor-made to eat with German mustard made by the country's *Senf Meisters* (master mustard makers). In the north and west of Germany the preference is for a sharper flavour, such as that made in Dusseldorf, which perfectly complements the flavour of rich dishes such as pork knuckle or full-flavoured sausages. In the south, particularly in Bavaria, a mild, sweet mustard is more popular and is often eaten with *wiesswurt* (veal sausage).

In Scandinavia the taste is for a mild, sweet mustard such as that used in gravadlax, the Swedish sauce traditionally eaten with cured salmon. This sauce is flavoured strongly with dill. In Denmark, a similar style of sauce accompanies roast goose.

The British love mustard with meats and fish of all kinds and frequently offer it with roast or grilled beef, hot or cold ham, pork pies and sausages. It is traditionally served with oily fish such as herrings and mackerel and it also partners hard cheese, such as Cheddar, in sandwiches or toasted into a Welsh rarebit. This rich dish of Cheddar cheese melted with ale, mustard and seasonings on toasted bread needs the addition of the mustard to give it "bite" and stop it being too cloying.

British palates adore pickles and chutneys. Mustard seed has always been a classic constituent of pickling spice, along with chillies, ginger and allspice to flavour the vinegar prior to pickling fruit or vegetables.

In Italy mustard takes on yet another form in the shape of *mostarda di frutta* (fruit flavoured with a syrup containing mustard oil or seed) with many different regional variations. There is *mostarda di Cremona*, including pears, apricots, cherries, plums, peaches, melons and figs, or *mostarda alla Toscana*, with apples and

Roast beef, traditionally served with mustard, is the national dish in Britain: it has earned the British the nickname "rostbifs" in France.

A wonderfully elaborate and beautifully decorated jar designed to hold the Italian speciality Mostarda di Frutta. Different regions of the country have their own specialities.

pears cooked in *vin santo*. This often accompanies *bollito misto*, the classic dish of boiled meats, or *zampona di Modena* (a boned pig's trotter stuffed with pork, bacon and truffles), ham, eels and cotechino (a spicy pork sausage) served with lentils. In Lombardy, where pasta vies with rice and polenta as a staple food, *mostarda di Cremona* is mixed with pumpkin to stuff a *tortelli di zucca*.

Yet another "mostarda" comes from the Veneto region, and is eaten with goose, baked ham or pork, while in Piedmont a local version of fruits and nuts in a syrup made from must from the Barbera grape accompanies Taleggio cheese or boiled meats. There is one very hot version, good with boiled meats, known as *mostarda di frutta piccante* and based on puréed fruits. Its origins are probably very old, from the days when sweet and sour flavours were used more often than now, but all these mostardas are certainly an original taste, in these days of international cuisine.

Although the Americans enjoy a wide variety of mustards, when it comes to hot dogs it must be the smooth, runny sweet "ball-park" type.

MUSTARD ON THE MOVE

Americans love to eat on the move and mustard goes with them, chiefly in hot dogs and hamburgers, but also in deli-style sandwiches such as pastrami on rye. The American style of mustard tends to be smooth, mild and quite sweet, with a texture that makes it easy to squirt along a frankfurter single-handed. But it does not only appear at the ball-park, and is equally effective in more traditional cooking.

Mustard was first brought to America with the early settlers and soon trails of golden flowers marked the places where the first pioneers had travelled. By the beginning of the twentieth century, mustard was commonplace in America, but not particularly popular, so Francis French, a New York State mustard manufacturer, set his plant superintendent the task of producing a really successful formula.

The tradition of pickling fresh vegetables in order to preserve them is widespread throughout the world, and mustard seeds are a favourite flavouring for the preserving liquid.

This he did, creating a mild, creamy mustard which by 1915 had made sales of a million dollars for the company. In 1926 French's sold out to Colman's and nowadays in the States there are over 50 brands of speciality mustard, from Russian style to extra hot Chinese, to suit every palate and every style of food.

A more traditional use of mustard can be found in the southern states, where Virginia hams are still stuffed with a combination of sweet peppers and various greens, such as cabbage and spinach, before being spiked with mustard seed and Tabasco sauce. Mustard seeds blend into Cajun seasoning along with stalwarts such as pepper, cayenne and garlic. In this region mustard greens are often cooked as a vegetable.

THE ORIENTAL APPROACH

A major characteristic of Indian cuisine involves the blending of different spices together, and mustard seed frequently appears in various styles of seasoning. This does not, however, add the pungency that might be expected – the seeds are heated, giving them a nutty quality, and once ground, a slight bitterness develops which is considered a digestive aid. In the south of India spice blends tend to be hotter than their northern counterparts, combining mustard seeds with hot favourites such as chillies, curry leaves, coriander, turmeric and ginger. Mustard seeds are also used whole to season various foods such as vegetables and pulses, and for preparing relishes and chutneys, which are served with Indian breads or to accompany main courses. Mustard seed oil is used, particularly in Bengal and Kashmir, as a cooking medium. Its pungency when raw is transformed through heating into a sweet, nutty flavour. Cooked mustard leaves are also served as a leaf.

Sri Lanka mustard seed is usually fried in oil, before being finely ground and blended with other spices to make curry powder. The seeds can also be used coarsely ground and sprinkled over food as an individual seasoning. Mustard paste, which is a combination of black and brown seeds with other ingredients such as vinegar, garlic, ginger and sugar, is served with meat stews and curries.

The Chinese mix water or vinegar with a powerful mustard powder to make a pungent sauce, served with deep-fried food such as egg rolls. They also combine it with other flavourings such as sesame oil, vinegar and chilli

to make dipping sauces. The mustard plant is also widely used, with numerous different leafy varieties which are also used for their roots – these are sometimes pickled and used in meat dishes.

Japanese mustard, *karashi*, is one of the principal flavourings placed on the dining table, alongside soy sauce, rice vinegar, pepper and wasabi (Japanese horseradish). *Karashi* is traditionally served with a slow-fried dish of pork cutlet coated in breadcrumbs and accompanied by cabbage. Japanese noodles are the fast food of the cuisine, and versions such as *Hiyashi-chuka* (cold ramen noodles with ham, vegetables, omelette and beansprouts) are served in a soy, sesame and vinegar sauce. The pickles eaten after a main course are often prepared using mustard and wasabi.

Chinese mustard is always freshly made before serving, and so retains its fiery flavour to add piquancy to egg rolls and other dim sum dishes.

Curry spice mixtures usually include mustard seeds, and mustard oil is popular for frying.

From the Seed to the Pot

The way mustard is made today scarcely varies from methods we know our ancestors used. Machines and technology made the job easier and faster, but the finished results are probably much the same now as they have always been.

The manufacture of mustard is highly sophisticated, as all food processing is today, but it has kept very much to its roots, with little change to the ingredients or the way they are manipulated into powdered or ready-made mustards. We may have a huge variety of speciality mustards to choose from, but the basic recipes are still adhered to and mustard is one of the few food stuffs which seems to have kept its quality and remained unadulterated. Strict codes and controls, particularly in France, have probably been partly responsible for this high standard, but it is interesting that we expect our mustard to taste as it has always done and not to be adapted or updated.

Although mustard seed is grown on a huge scale worldwide and the industry is vast, the processes of harvesting, threshing, grinding and blending, while mechanized, are still the same as they always have been, and the mustard in the pot tastes as delicious as ever.

The ground seed is ready to be mixed with liquids or dry ingredients and blended into different types of mustard.

The mustard seeds must be harvested at exactly the right stage of ripeness and before the seeds begin to fall.

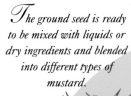

For some mustards which require a smoother texture, the husks around the seed are removed.

Depending on how they will be used, the seeds are ground to flour or just lightly crushed.

The tiny seeds are threshed from the small, dry pea-like pods and are checked for quality before being sieved to remove debris.

The seeds must be dried, either in old-fashioned stooks or in modern kilns, to the right degree of moisture.

It is often easy to for that a delicio sophisticated mustard o it all to a humble wh brown or black se

CHAPTER ONE

STARTERS

Any first course should be piquant and delicious, light and stimulating. Mustard has all the right qualities to add just what is needed to such dishes. Popular with cheese and eggs, subtle in soups, and powerful with more robust flavours, it starts any meal off with great style.

STARTERS

Mustard is the perfect instant flavouring for many quick and simple starters. It can be added straight from the jar to dressings, sauces, soups and all manner of fresh light dishes to start a meal or to make a snack. Crudités with a dip or sauce are perennially popular. Provide mild whole-grain mustards or mayonnaise flavoured with mustard as a dip, and a selection of the freshest raw vegetables arranged on a serving dish. Salad dressings are transformed by the imaginative use of seasonings, particularly by the careful addition of mustard. Give a new twist to grated carrot in a lemony dressing by finishing it with a sprinkling of black mustard seeds heated in a little oil until they pop, to make a refreshing salad with an Indian savour. Fish and shellfish have long been favourite starters. Gravadlax or marinated salmon has become a fashionable alternative to smoked salmon; a mustard and dill sauce, slightly sweet and quite thick, marries beautifully with the fish.

Two men and a woman pouring wine, *Velasquez, 1618*

CELERIAC SOUP *with* THYME-INFUSED PISTACHIOS

Hearty enough for a family supper, this easy-to-make soup is sufficiently sophisticated in flavour to offer to dinner party guests. The thyme-infused pistachios sprinkled on top add a distinctive quality which can be used to elevate many other soups. Stirred in at the last moment, the mustard imparts quite a strong flavour; add just one tablespoon and taste before adding a second.

SERVES 4

1 celeriac (about 500g • 1lb)
30g • 1oz butter
1 onion, chopped
1 leek, sliced
700ml • 1¼pt vegetable or chicken stock
2tsp vegetable oil

20g • ¾oz shelled pistachio nuts, roughly chopped
1 sprig thyme, roughly chopped
200ml • 7fl oz milk
salt and freshly ground black pepper
5tbsp double cream
1-2tbsp wholegrain mustard

Preheat the oven to 180°C/375°F/gas mark 4.

Roughly chop the celeriac, placing the pieces in water to prevent discoloration.

Melt the butter in a large saucepan over a medium heat, add the onion and leek and sauté for about 2 minutes until soft. Add the chopped celeriac and sauté for a further minute. Pour in the stock, bring to the boil and simmer for 10 minutes, or until the celeriac is tender.

Meanwhile, to infuse the chopped pistachio nuts with the thyme, pour the oil into a small roasting pan and heat over a high heat. Put the pistachio nuts and the thyme into the pan and roast in the oven for about 4 minutes.

Remove the cooked vegetables from the heat and allow to cool slightly. Purée them in a food processor and return to a clean pan. Add the milk, season and heat through.

Stir the cream and mustard into the soup and gently heat through. Serve the soup sprinkled with the thyme-infused pistachio nuts.

CRUDITÉS *with* MUSTARD DIPS

A common hors d'oeuvre of the French countryside, crudités (raw vegetables) are an excellent and easy way to enjoy fresh, healthy fare. The selection of dips given here provides a range of mustardy flavours to accompany the crudités. The nutty dip is inspired by a sophisticated sauce recipe devised in ancient Rome.

SERVES 4

4 carrots, peeled and cut into strips
4 sticks celery, cut into strips
1 bunch spring onions, each trimmed and cut in half
1 small cauliflower, broken into florets
½ cucumber, cut in half across and then into strips
8 cherry tomatoes, halved

AUBERGINE DIP
1 aubergine (about 250g • 8oz)
1 head garlic, unpeeled
1tbsp French mustard
2tbsp olive oil

salt and freshly ground black pepper

MUSTARD DIP
6tbsp natural yoghurt
6tbsp sour cream
2tbsp wholegrain mustard
1tbsp chopped fresh tarragon, or 1tsp dried tarragon

NUTTY DIP
30g • 1oz pine nuts, finely ground
30g • 1oz ground almonds
1tsp English mustard
3tbsp olive oil
4tbsp fromage frais

To make the Mustard Dip and the Nutty Dip, combine the ingredients for each dip in a bowl.

To make the Aubergine Dip, preheat the oven to 200°C/400°F/gas mark 6. Prick the skin of the aubergine in several places, place it on a baking tray with the head of garlic and bake in the preheated oven for 25 minutes. When the aubergine is cooked, remove the tray from the oven and allow the aubergine to cool slightly before carefully removing the skin. Squeeze the garlic purée from the cooked cloves. Place the aubergine flesh in a food processor, add half of the garlic purée and the remaining ingredients, and mix well. (The unused half of the purée can be mixed into soups, sauces or used as a sandwich spread.)

To serve, transfer each dip to a small clean dish, place them in the centre of a serving platter and arrange all the raw vegetables around. Alternatively, arrange a selection of vegetables on individual dishes with some of each dip on the side.

The clear, fresh flavours and crisp textures of recently harvested and prepared vegetables highlight mustard's subtleties and depths.

SPICY CRAB CLAWS

This is a wonderfully messy dish to serve to your guests. Provide plenty of finger bowls and paper napkins and invite your friends to tuck in. If the claws still have their shells, you will need crackers and picks for digging out the last bits of meat. The mustard adds heat, reinforcing the effect of the chilli peppers.

SERVES 4

2tbsp vegetable oil	*1x 200g • 7oz can chopped*
4 shallots, finely chopped	*tomatoes*
1 clove garlic, crushed	*1tsp English mustard*
2 red chilli peppers, finely	*salt and freshly ground black*
chopped	*pepper*
300ml • ½pt fish or vegetable	*16-24 crab claws, depending*
stock	*on size*
	1 loaf crusty bread, optional

Heat the oil in a large saucepan, put in the shallots, garlic and chilli peppers and gently cook for about 4 minutes until soft but not browned.

Pour in the stock and add the chopped tomatoes. Stir in the mustard, season and then bring to the boil. Add the crab claws, reduce the heat and simmer for 3 minutes.

Using a slotted spoon, remove the crab claws to either a large serving dish or four individual dishes. Pour the spicy sauce over the top and serve immediately. Provide plenty of crusty bread for mopping up any leftover sauce.

>>>>>>>> <<<<<<<<

MINI CHICKEN KEBABS *cooked in a* MUSTARD MARINADE

The unmistakable mustardy flavour of these dainty kebabs will delight all mustard lovers. Marinating the chicken in yoghurt helps to tenderize it, with the result that the cooked kebabs really melt in the mouth. Soak 8-10 small wooden kebab sticks in water for 10 minutes before using to prevent them from burning.

SERVES 4

150ml · 5fl oz natural yoghurt
1 lime, juice only
salt and freshly ground black
   pepper

3 chicken breasts, skinned and
   boned
2tbsp coarse grain mustard
selection of salad leaves
lime wedges for garnish

In a bowl, combine 3 tablespoons of the yoghurt with the lime juice and season with salt and black pepper. Cut the chicken breasts into 2.5cm/1in cubes and mix into the yoghurt and lime mixture. Cover and leave to marinate for 2 hours.

Meanwhile, combine the remaining yoghurt with the mustard and some black pepper to make a basting mixture. Heat the grill to medium.

Remove the chicken from the marinade and thread the pieces on to small kebab sticks. Grill the kebabs on one side for 5 minutes. Turn, baste generously with the mustard mixture and grill for a further 5 minutes. Increase the heat to high, turn the kebabs once more, baste again and grill for 5 minutes more, or until the chicken is cooked.

Serve with a selection of salad leaves and garnish with lime wedges.

THREE-CHEESE TARTLETS

As well as being ideal starters, these tartlets can be served at buffets or taken on a picnic. The mustard flavour is intense, but you can reduce the amount of mustard if you prefer.

SERVES 4

SHORTCRUST PASTRY
90g · 3oz flour
pinch salt
45g · 1½oz firm margarine or
   butter, diced
FILLING
30g · 1oz butter
1 red onion, thinly sliced
1 size 3 egg, beaten
125ml · 4fl oz milk
1tbsp honey

2tbsp coarse grain mustard
30g · 1oz crumbled Dolcelatte
   cheese
30g · 1oz freshly grated
   Parmesan cheese
30g · 1oz chopped Bel Paese
   cheese
salt and freshly ground black
   pepper
selection of lettuce leaves

First make the shortcrust pastry. Sieve the flour into a bowl with the salt. Add the diced margarine or butter and cut through the flour with a knife. When each piece of butter is coated with flour, rub into the flour with your fingertips only until the mixture resembles fine breadcrumbs. Add 1½ tablespoons of water and bring the mixture together to form a ball of dough. Chill in the refrigerator, covered, for at least 30 minutes.

Remove the chilled pastry from the refrigerator, allow it to stand 10 minutes then roll it out to about 0.5cm/¼in thick. Cut out pastry circles large enough to line four 10cm/4in diameter tartlet tins. Line the tins with the pastry and prick the base of each circle a few times with a fork. Chill the lined tins for 30 minutes; this allows the pastry to relax and prevents shrinkage during cooking.

Meanwhile, make the filling. Melt the butter in a saucepan and add the sliced onion. Cook over a medium-low heat for 20 minutes, stirring occasionally to ensure the onions remain evenly coated with butter.

Preheat the oven to 190°C/375°F/gas mark 5. Place a few baking beans or scrunched up foil in the base of each tartlet and bake them blind for 6 minutes.

Combine all the remaining filling ingredients except for the lettuce with the caramelized onions. Push down any tartlet base that has risen with the back of a spoon. Fill each tartlet to just below the rim with the filling and bake for 20-25 minutes until the tops are golden brown and the filling has set.

Serve each tartlet on a bed of salad leaves.

WELSH RAREBIT SOUFFLÉ

This inspired soufflé incorporates the essential elements of a traditional Welsh Rarebit – cheese, ale and mustard. Ask your guests to take their places before taking the soufflé out of the oven as it will sink very quickly once removed. You can use this recipe to make either one large soufflé or four individual ones.

SERVES 4

*30g • 1oz butter, plus extra for
  greasing
15g • ½oz fresh breadcrumbs
30g • 1oz plain flour
4tbsp milk*

*3tbsp beer or ale
60g • 2oz grated mature
  Cheddar cheese
3 size 3 eggs, separated
2tbsp English mustard*

Preheat the oven to 190°C/375°F/gas mark 5. Grease the soufflé dish or four individual ramekins with butter and sprinkle the bottom and sides with the breadcrumbs.

Melt the butter in a saucepan, add the flour and mix well. Pour in the milk gradually, stirring to prevent any lumps from forming. Stir in the beer and grated cheese. Remove from the heat and add the egg yolks and the mustard.

Whisk the egg whites until they form soft peaks. A good test to ensure they are sufficiently beaten is to hold the beaters upright with some mixture on them; the mixture should remain firm but with the top of the peak drooping slightly.

Add one tablespoon of whisked egg white to the sauce and fold in. Gently fold in the remaining egg white.

Pour the soufflé mixture into the prepared dish or ramekins and bake in the centre of the oven for 18-20 minutes for a large dish or 8-10 minutes for individual ones. The soufflé should be golden brown on top and will be slightly moist in the centre.

Celtic Treat

Welsh rabbit, confusingly, contains no meat, but is simply melted cheese on hot buttered toast. (Rarebit is a fanciful coinage dating from the eighteenth century.) And mustard is a vital ingredient, not only because the flavours of cheese and mustard complement each other so well; the mustard also acts as an emulsifier, preventing the fat from separating out of cheese as it cooks, and so stabilizing the mixture.

GOUJONS *of* PLAICE *with* MUSTARD *and* HERB CRUST

The inspiration behind this dish is the herbed breadcrumb coating devised by a resourceful fourteenth-century chef for an impromptu chicken supper when he and his master, France's King Charles VI, were campaigning near Sainte-Menehould. A mustard sauce accompanied that dish, but here the mustard is incorporated into the coating which translates admirably to white fish. Lemon wedges, a crisp salad and one or two of the dipping sauces, such as those on pages 66 and 67, complement the goujons.

SERVES 4

750g • 1½lb plaice fillets
3 size 3 eggs, beaten
3tsp English mustard
150g • 5oz fresh breadcrumbs

3tbsp mixed fresh herbs, finely
  chopped (such as parsley,
  thyme, oregano)
vegetable oil for deep frying.

Wash and pat dry the plaice fillets and cut them into thin strips about 12cm/5in long by 1cm/½in thick.

Combine the beaten eggs and mustard in a bowl. In another bowl combine the breadcrumbs and herbs. Dip each strip of fish into the egg mixture and then into the breadcrumb mixture.

Pour oil into a frying pan until it is 7.5cm/3in deep and heat it until a cube of bread dropped in sizzles and immediately floats to the surface. Deep-fry the goujons in batches for about 2 minutes until crisp and golden, gently moving them around with a spatula to ensure even cooking. Drain the goujons on kitchen paper then serve.

GRUYÈRE *and* HAM CROISSANTS

Coarse grain mustard makes its own strong, crunchy contribution to this light but satisfying snack while binding together the flavours of the other ingredients. Quick and easy to prepare, the filled croissants can be served as part of a brunch, for a light lunch, or for afternoon high tea.

SERVES 4

125g • 4oz grated Gruyère cheese	*4 croissants*
	butter, optional
4 slices ham, roughly chopped	*mixed salad leaves for garnish*
1½tbsp coarse grain mustard	

Place the cheese, ham and mustard in a bowl and mix well. Slice open the croissants, warm under the grill and spread with butter if using. Fill each croissant generously with the cheese mixture.

Serve with a generous garnish of fresh mixed salad leaves.

>>>>>

Hot Dogs

Hot Dogs are as traditionally American as apple pie. They first appeared in the 1920s, and a popular cartoon of the time featuring a dachshund helped to fix the name in the public's imagination. And no true American would eat a hot dog without a liberal helping of bright yellow, mild, slightly sweet mustard. The mustard flows over the sausage then seeps into the bread. As the eater bites into the "dog", the mustard oozes out of the sides of the roll, leaving a yellow tide mark around the mouth. This is cleared by a well-practised lick of the tongue.

SALMON GRAVADLAX *with a* MUSTARD SAUCE

Gravadlax (salmon cured in salt, dill and peppercorns) is an essential ingredient of the Scandinavian smorgasbord. In less grand presentations, humble bread and butter is the ideal accompaniment. The dish takes some time to cure but is well worth the wait.

SERVES 4

750g • 1½lb fresh salmon, middle cut, halved along the backbone, backbone and other bones removed
1 large bunch dill
1tbsp sugar
3tbsp coarse sea salt
1tbsp crushed peppercorns

MUSTARD SAUCE
2tbsp whole grain mustard
1tbsp sugar
2tbsp white wine vinegar
4tbsp olive oil
freshly chopped dill
salt and freshly ground black pepper

Scrape the scales off the salmon and pat it dry with kitchen towel.

Place a handful of dill on a large plate and place one half of the salmon on top, skin side down. Combine the sugar, salt and peppercorns and sprinkle over the salmon. Add another handful of dill and cover with the remaining salmon half, skin side up. Cover with the remaining dill. Cover the entire plate with film and place a plate on top, weighted down with a heavy object. Place in the refrigerator for at least 48 hours but not more than 3 days. Baste the salmon twice each day with the juices produced, separating the salmon halves slightly to baste inside them.

To make the mustard sauce, combine the mustard, sugar and vinegar in a bowl. Gradually add the oil, beating continuously. Add the dill and salt and pepper to taste.

When ready to serve, remove the salmon from the refrigerator, scrape clean and pat dry. Slice thinly using a sharp knife and avoiding the skin; slice from left to right or right to left rather than from top to bottom.

Serve with the mustard sauce.

Mustard Pots

Because mustard has always been used as a table condiment to serve with food, as well as an ingredient in the kitchen, there have always been containers specially designed to hold it. By the eighteenth century, exquisite examples of cruet sets were being produced by master craftsmen. The three main condiments were catered for – salt, pepper and mustard. In today's less formal world, we are likely to just put the mustard pot straight on the table, but in the more leisurely and genteel days of, say, two centuries ago, the freshly made-up mustard would be spooned into a little blue glass dish and stood inside a gleaming silver mustard pot.

In the Middle Ages mustard was sold in narrow-necked jars, to keep as much air as possible from reaching the mustard. Parchment was stretched over the top and tightly tied, to keep evaporation to a minimum. No doubt these jars were put straight on the table in all but the grandest households. However, domestic pots were being made even then, usually from pewter. Over the next few hundred years other materials began to be used for pots – gold plate or silver for the rich, and glass, china or porcelain for everyone else. It is possible that mustard spoons made from animal horn first appeared around the same time. Horn mustard spoons can still be bought today. The smooth, natural material seems exactly right for the purpose, never tainting the mustard or tarnishing, as silver would.

The history and development of commercial French mustard pots is fascinating; they slowly changed shape as manufacturing methods changed and modernized and the need for good seals was realized. Some of the oldest pots are simple and beautiful, always with a narrow neck and invariably with printed or written details of the place of origin and type of mustard. By the twentieth century, all kinds of inventive containers had been introduced as a means of boosting sales and attracting new customers. In France, mustard was often packed in small, reusable tumblers which could be cleaned and used on the table for water once empty. In Britain, mustard pots have been turned into money boxes and other novelties in the past and early mechanical cigarette lighters were even made from Colman's mustard boxes.

The French mustard producer Antoine Maille offered nearly a hundred different mustards to his clients and these pots, dated 1747, were from a period of great success for his company. The simple, peasant style of decoration was then very popular.

A silver mustard pot with a hinged lid and its own spoon. The lid was important, to prevent air darkening the mustard and forming a skin on it. Even so, mustard had to be freshly made up each day.

The handles on this nineteenth-century pot are unusual, but the basic shape is the familiar one which has remained unchanged for centuries.

A fine, elegant Georgian silver mustard pot on decorative legs. No doubt it would have been part of a set, including a salt-dish in the same style, but without a lid, and a pepper grinder.

53

Mustard spoons were usually in keeping with the style of the pot. A wooden spoon was common for everyday use.

A large-scale earthenware hand-decorated French mustard jar from the 18th century. This shape, with a narrow neck and bulbous sides, was traditional and remained the same whatever the size of the pot.

CHAPTER TWO

SALADS

ood salads need a light hand and sensitive touch to compose them and an eye for colourful but tasty combinations. The most important part though, is always the dressing. Whether this is a creamy mayonnaise or pungent vinaigrette, mustard is the key element in creating a delicious result.

SALADS

Far removed from the usual combination of lettuce, tomato and cucumber, a salad today is likely to be the star dish of a meal with ingredients ranging from grilled vegetables, earthy pulses, fresh shellfish or unusual cheeses. But, however excitingly the salad is put together, it will need a good dressing, and good dressings need mustard.

A carefully made vinaigrette with grainy mustard can turn a plateful of salad leaves into a full-scale meal. Add a sprinkling of other ingredients such as crisp grilled bacon in little strips or melted goats cheese, or leave the mixed leaves plain and simple. Use the best oil and wine vinegar or lemon juice you can lay your hands on and have fun choosing an appropriate mustard.

Still life with asparagus, *Louis Moillon, 1630*

>>>>>>>><<<<<<<<

Warm Roasted Vegetable Salad

A mustard dressing seems to bring out the best in vegetables, especially when they are served warm. As well as being a substantial accompaniment to a main meal, this warm salad can be served as a starter. The crispy herb croutons should be added at the last moment to prevent them from soaking up too much dressing. Allow time to prepare the aubergine before you make the salad.

SERVES 4

1 aubergine
salt
6tbsp olive oil
2 red sweet peppers, seeded and cut into eighths
2 courgettes, cut into 2.5cm • 1in rounds
2 small red onions, peeled and cut into eighths
1 small bunch thyme
freshly ground black pepper
3 cloves garlic, cut in half
1tbsp freshly chopped oregano, or 2tsp dried oregano

4 slices white bread, crusts removed and cut into 1cm • ½in cubes
1 Italian mozzarella cheese, torn into small pieces
60g • 2oz whole black olives, such as kalamata

DRESSING

4tbsp extra virgin olive oil
1tbsp balsamic vinegar
1tbsp lemon juice
1tsp Dijon mustard
salt and freshly ground black pepper

Cut the aubergine in half lengthways and sprinkle with salt. Leave for at least 1 hour then rinse under cold water, peel and cut into 2.5cm/1in cubes.

Preheat the oven to 200°C/400°F/gas mark 6.

Pour 4 tablespoons of the olive oil into a large roasting pan and heat over a high heat on a hob. Add the aubergines, sweet peppers, courgettes and onions and mix well. Add the thyme, some salt and plenty of freshly ground black pepper. Cover with foil, place in the oven and roast for about 30 minutes. Remove the pan from the oven, turn all the vegetables and return to the oven. Roast, uncovered, for a further 30 minutes until cooked.

Meanwhile, combine all the dressing ingredients in a bowl and mix well. Rub the sides of the serving dish with two of the garlic halves then discard them.

Remove the cooked vegetables from the oven and transfer to a serving dish. Then make the croutons. Heat the remaining olive oil in a frying pan over a high heat, fry the remaining garlic halves for 1 minute then discard the garlic.

Put the cubes of bread in the pan with the chopped oregano and fry for about 2 minutes, shaking the pan frequently, until the croutons are golden brown.

Toss the mozzarella pieces and olives through the vegetables, pour the dressing over and top with the croutons.

Temples to Mustard

The Mount Horeb Mustard Museum, in Mount Horeb, Wisconsin, USA, houses the largest collection of mustards in the world. It was opened in 1989 by its curator, Barry Levenson, with just 365 mustards. By January 1995 the number had risen to over 2,000, including examples from such far-flung places as Guatemala and Siberia. The Museum has its own wittily informative and practical newsletter, The Proper Mustard. It also sells mustards and mustard paraphenalia such as mustard cookbooks, pots, T-shirts, mugs and toy cars and even has its own university-style pennant.

Colman's Mustard Shop and Museum in Bridewell Alley, Norwich, England, is very different. Established in 1973 as part of the 150th anniversary celebrations of the founding of the firm, it concentrates on the considerable role of Colman's in the history of mustard production. It contains displays of traditional mustard production methods, and sells a range of mustards and associated products, such as pots, aprons and so on, bearing the company name.

SUMMER SALAD BOWL

A glass serving bowl is an ideal way to show off this layered salad as a centrepiece. If you want to make the salad in advance of serving, coat the avocado slices with lemon juice as you cut them to prevent discolouration.

SERVES 4

¼ red cabbage, shredded
½ crispy lettuce, shredded or torn
1 carrot, grated
1 beefsteak tomato, sliced
1 red onion, thinly sliced
1 avocado, stone removed, peeled, and thinly sliced

DRESSING
150ml · 5fl oz natural yoghurt
1tsp coarse grain mustard
4tbsp olive oil
2tbsp white wine vinegar
salt and freshly ground black pepper

Layer up a large serving bowl (with an approximate capacity of 2 litres/3½pt) with the raw vegetables to make contrasting bands of colour.

Combine all the dressing ingredients in a bowl and pour evenly over the top of the salad. Allow the dressing to filter through for about 10 minutes before serving.

60

ROAST BEEF SALAD
with MUSTARD SAUCE

The sauce in this recipe is quite piquant. If, when you taste it, you would prefer a milder version, add two tablespoons of sour cream and mix well.

SERVES 4

2tbsp mayonnaise
1tbsp French mustard
2tsp creamed horseradish
1tbsp lemon juice
20 pitted black olives (about 45g · 1½oz), roughly chopped

4 spring onions, thinly sliced
freshly ground black pepper
12 thin slices cooked roast beef (about 375g · 12oz)
1 bunch watercress, washed and trimmed

With the exception of the roast beef and the watercress, combine all the ingredients together in a bowl to make the sauce.

Divide the watercress among four plates, arrange 3 slices of roast beef on top and spoon some sauce over.

>><<

Growing Your Own Mustard and Cress

To grow the sweet and slightly peppery salad garnish, mustard and cress, use white mustard seeds, brassica alba, *and garden cress,* lepidium sativum. *It is fun, and very easy, to grow them in shapes, as in the playing card symbols shown here. Simply place a template of your chosen design on damp soil in a shallow tray, or on a damp cloth, cotton wool or paper tissues, and press firmly to make an indentation. Then sprinkle a thin layer of mustard seeds in the shape. Three to four days later sow the cress seeds. Keep them moist. After two weeks they should be about 5 cm/2 inches long, when they are ready to eat.*

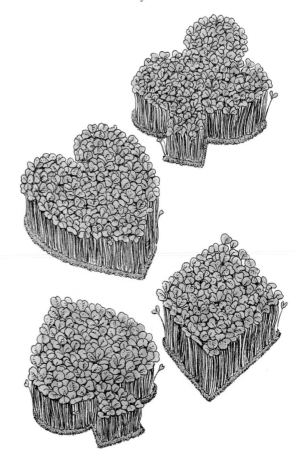

FRUITY DUCK SALAD

Barbary duck, which is leaner and has a more mature flavour than other breeds, is particularly suited to the lively ingredients of this dish, but if it is unavailable any breed of duck can be used. As the mustard content is quite high, giving a strong savour, the decision as to exactly how much to include is a matter of personal taste. The dish may be served warm or cold.

SERVES 4

3 oranges, juice only
1 lime, juice only
1tbsp soy sauce
2-3 Barbary duck breasts
    (about 600g • 1¼lb),
    with skin

75g • 2½oz dried apricots
1-1½tbsp whole grain mustard,
    according to taste
freshly ground black pepper
selection of salad leaves

Combine the orange and lime juices with the soy sauce in a bowl. Using a sharp knife, make 3 or 4 shallow incisions across the fleshy sides of the duck breasts. Place the duck breasts in the citrus juice and soy mixture, cover with film and leave to marinate for 4-5 hours.

Meanwhile, place the apricots in a bowl, pour over sufficient boiling water to cover and leave to soak for 10 minutes. Purée the softened apricots with the soaking water either in a food processor or by passing them through a sieve. Mix in the mustard and black pepper.

Remove the duck breasts from the marinade, reserving the latter, and place under a hot grill. Grill for 5-6 minutes on each side, basting a few times with the reserved marinade. The grilling time will vary according to the size of the duck breasts; test by cutting a small slice from the end of one breast to see if it is done to your liking. Remove from the grill and allow to cool slightly. Remove the skin and slice each breast thinly.

Add about 6 tablespoons of the reserved marinade to the apricot sauce and mix well.

To serve, arrange the duck slices on a selection of salad leaves with a portion of apricot sauce by the side.

Mixed Tomato Salad *with* Mustard Dressing

In summer months, many varieties of tomato become available making it possible to create a visually stimulating salad. A good mix might be one beefsteak, eight yellow and/or red cherry tomatoes and six others, including perhaps flavia, but it does depend on what you can find. As the tomatoes in the shops tend not to be fully ripened, buy them a week in advance and let them finish ripening at home.

SERVES 4

750g-1kg • 1½-2lb selection of ripe tomatoes	2tsp coarse grain mustard tarragon
6tbsp extra virgin olive oil	salt and freshly ground black pepper
2tbsp balsamic vinegar	
1tbsp freshly squeezed lime juice	2tbsp chopped fresh tarragon,
1 clove garlic, quartered	or 2tsp dried

Cut any large tomatoes into eighths, medium-sized ones into quarters and cherry tomatoes in half.

Combine all the remaining ingredients except for the tarragon and mix well. Pour the dressing over the tomatoes, ensuring that they are completely coated. Sprinkle the tarragon over and serve.

>><<

Seeds of War

Alexander III (356–323 BC), also known as Alexander the Great, was one of the greatest generals in history. He laid the foundations for the Hellenistic world of territorial kingdoms, and in the process became a legendary hero. One of his greatest conquests was the defeat of the Persian empire in a series of battles. During one of them, in 335 BC, Alexander was sent a bag of mustard seeds by Darius II, Emperor of Persia. The quantity of the seeds symbolized the enormous number of troops under his command. Alexander responded by sending back a bag of mustard seeds, to show his fiery strength of purpose.

It was in the year 1760 that a
superior of the ancient
religious order of Meaux
transmitted to the
Pommery family the
secret recipe of
their marvelous
specialty
"Moutarde des
Chanoines", the
Abbot's Mustard.
This mustard has been
served at the tables of the
kings of France since 1632.

Mustard Pom

PRODUCT OF FRANCE

MOUTARDE de MEA
POMMERY
AROMATISÉE AU VIN

NET WT

>>>>>>>><<<<<<<<

ORANGE *and* BEAN SPROUT SALAD

Roasted pumpkin seeds give this refreshing, crunchy salad a wonderful smoky flavour while the mustard in the dressing stands up manfully to the strong flavour of the oranges. Crisp and colourful, it is a perfect dish for lunch in the garden on a hot summer's day.

SERVES 4

200g • 7oz fresh bean sprouts
200g • 7oz rocket, stemmed, washed, dried and torn
90g • 3oz selection of salad leaves, washed, dried and torn
2 oranges
30g • 1oz pumpkin seeds

DRESSING

1tbsp freshly squeezed orange juice
½tsp freshly grated ginger
1tbsp white wine vinegar
5tbsp olive oil
2tsp honey
1½tbsp coarse grain mustard
salt and freshly ground black pepper

Preheat the oven to 200°C/400°F/gas mark 6.

In a large bowl, mix the bean sprouts, rocket and salad leaves together. Remove the peel and pith from the oranges and cut into segments.

Place the pumpkin seeds on a baking tray and roast in the oven for 5 minutes.

Mix all the dressing ingredients together, pour over the bean sprouts and salad leaves and toss thoroughly. Scatter the orange segments on top and sprinkle the freshly roasted pumpkin seeds over them.

MUSTARDY POTATO SALAD

Mustard is an essential ingredient of a good potato salad and here it holds its own with the other highly flavoured ingredients. Small new potatoes are especially delicious, but when they are unavailable medium potatoes, cut into quarters, are fine. Although not vital, making this dish in advance gives the potatoes time to soak up the spicy sauce.

SERVES 4

625g • 1¼lb small new potatoes (approximately 20), washed but not peeled
1tbsp English mustard
½tsp hot pepper sauce
4tbsp olive oil

2tbsp tomato purée
1 clove garlic, crushed
2tbsp chopped fresh oregano
1tbsp freshly squeezed lime juice
salt and freshly ground black pepper

Place the potatoes in a saucepan of cold water, bring to the boil then simmer for 10-15 minutes, or until tender.

Meanwhile, make the mustard dressing. Combine all the remaining ingredients in a small bowl.

Drain the cooked potatoes, rinse under cold water and drain again. Transfer to a large bowl, pour over the dressing and mix well.

65

Mustard Sayings

According to Eric Partridge, the British lexicographer, in his Dictionary of Slang, *the phrase "cut the mustard" means to succeed in performing or accomplishing something, hence to be of importance. He traces the first usage to 1904, when the phrase "up to the mustard", or up to the mark, was also in use. The related expression "to be mustard at" also suggested excellence, but by the 1920s this phrase took on sexual connotations and was altogether more suggestive.* The Dictionary of American Slang, *however, maintains that "cut the mustard" entered the English language in the early 1900s from Philadelphia, where it was said that "groups have special vested interests. And that's not gonna cut the mustard."*

CRUNCHY COLESLAW

Although caraway seeds normally have an intense flavour, their effect in this recipe is tamed by the presence of the mustard. If the coleslaw is allowed to stand, however, the caraway could eventually dominate as the strength of mustard weakens with time. Therefore, you may wish to reduce the quantity of caraway seeds by one teaspoon if you make the coleslaw several hours in advance.

SERVES 4

¼ red cabbage, roughly chopped
¼ white cabbage, roughly chopped
2 carrots, grated
2 sticks celery, chopped

60g • 2oz roughly chopped pecans
3tbsp sour cream
2tbsp natural yoghurt
2tsp caraway seeds
1tbsp English mustard
2tsp honey

Put the red and white cabbage, the grated carrots, chopped celery and chopped pecans into a large bowl and mix well.

Combine the remaining ingredients, pour over the vegetables and pecans and mix thoroughly.

DRESSING & SAUCES

WHEN USED IN DRESSINGS AND SAUCES MUSTARD PLAYS
AN IMPORTANT PART IN THE RECIPE AS IT PROVIDES NOT ONLY FLAVOUR
BUT ALSO ACTS AS A THICKENER.

1. CORIANDER DRESSING

This fragrant, summery dressing will enhance any salad.

1tbsp whole grain mustard
5tbsp olive oil
2tbsp raspberry wine vinegar
2tbsp roughly chopped fresh
  coriander, plus extra for garnish
freshly ground black pepper

Combine all the ingredients in a bowl and serve with any salad selection.

2. HERB AND MUSTARD DRESSING

A versatile salad dressing for all occasions.

2tsp whole grain mustard
4tbsp hazelnut oil
2tbsp tarragon vinegar
1tbsp finely chopped fresh tarragon
salt and freshly ground black pepper

Combine all the ingredients in a bowl and serve with a selection of salad ingredients.

3. SPICY DRESSING

If this dressing is made up a few days in advance, its piquancy intensifies.

3tbsp olive oil
1tbsp white wine vinegar
1tsp chilli powder
1tsp mustard powder
1 small red chilli pepper,
  finely chopped
1 clove garlic, crushed
1tbsp fresh lime juice
freshly ground black pepper

Place all the ingredients in a jar and shake well until combined.

4. MUSTARDY HOLLANDAISE SAUCE

In this sauce, which is traditionally served with fish, the mustard acts as a stabilizer to prevent curdling.

2 size 3 eggs, yolks only
2tsp vinegar or lemon juice
125g • 4oz butter, cut into small pieces
2tsp mustard powder
salt

Place the egg yolks, 1 teaspoon of the vinegar or lemon juice with 1 tablespoon of water in a double boiler or in a bowl set over a pan of simmering water (the bowl must not touch the water). Whisk the ingredients together until the yolks just begin to thicken and the mixture clings to the whisk when it is lifted from the bowl. Continue whisking, adding the butter to the bowl 1 piece at a time, making sure each piece is thoroughly incorporated before adding the next.

    When all the butter is incorporated and the sauce is thick and creamy, add the mustard powder, salt to taste and the remaining teaspoon of vinegar or lemon juice.

5. ALL-PURPOSE MUSTARD SAUCE

This all-rounder goes well with all meat and vegetable dishes.

30g • 1oz butter
1½ tbsp flour
250ml • 8fl oz milk
2tsp mustard powder, or 1tbsp Dijon mustard
salt and freshly ground black pepper
2tbsp single cream, optional

Melt the butter in a saucepan over a high heat. Stir in the flour and cook for 1 minute. Lower the heat and pour in the milk gradually, stirring as you pour to prevent lumps forming. Add the mustard, salt and freshly ground black pepper and the cream, if using. Bring the mixture to the boil then serve.

CHAPTER THREE

MAIN COURSES

Mustard takes centre stage in many classic main course recipes, where its close affinity to fish and meat is shown at its best. Use it to crust the skin of a char-grilled fish or to make a quick sauce for steak. Try something more adventurous such as richly glazed pork or subtle spiced Indian lamb.

Main Courses

The versatility of mustard as a flavouring is seen at its best in main course dishes. It can be used to marinate, to baste, to season, to coat, to stuff and to sauce, or maybe eaten simply as part of a relish alongside a finished dish.

Many cuisines feature recipes for various meats cooked in mustard-flavoured sauces, ranging from those for rabbit and chicken, such as lapin Dijonnaise, *to much stronger flavoured kidneys and cuts of beef. Sausages, however well seasoned, lack a certain something without mustard to eat with them, and the famous American hot dog, usually a mix of pork and beef, is invariably served with a large squirt of mustard. Germany has dozens of sausage specialities eaten hot with mustard and steaming piles of sauerkraut or mashed potatoes and washed down with delicious German beer.*

Mustardy mayonnaise is delicious with many foods, from simple baked potatoes to a warm salad of baby leeks.

>>>>>>>><<<<<<<<

From Chronique D'Angleterre, *late fifteenth century*

FINGER-LICKING SPARE RIBS

These ribs are quite simply delicious! For crispy ribs, cook them in the oven without basting. If you prefer moister ribs, either grill or bake them, basting several times with the marinade during the cooking. The ribs can also be cooked on a barbecue.

SERVES 4

12 spare ribs (about	*2tsp chilli powder*
1.25kg · 2½lb)	*1 lime, juice only*
MARINADE	*2tbsp whole grain mustard*
90ml · 3fl oz soy sauce	*90g · 3oz dried apricots,*
60ml · 2fl oz rice vinegar	*soaked in hot water for*
4 cloves garlic, crushed	*10 minutes if necessary (see*
2.5cm · 1in piece fresh root	*packet instructions)*
ginger, grated	*60g · 2oz soft brown sugar*

Place all the marinade ingredients, except for the soft brown sugar, in a food processor and process to a smooth purée. Mix in the sugar carefully, but do not blend as this would result in the marinade becoming too runny.

Place the ribs side by side in a shallow dish, in a single layer if possible, and pour over the marinade, ensuring the ribs are evenly coated. Cover and place in the refrigerator for 24-48 hours to marinate, the longer the better. Turn the ribs several times whilst marinating.

Remove the ribs from the refrigerator at least 30 minutes before cooking. Preheat the oven to 200°C/400°F/gas mark 6, if required for baking the ribs.

Remove the ribs from the marinade, reserving the marinade for basting if desired. For crispy ribs, bake them in the oven for 30-40 minutes. For moist ribs bake them in the oven for 15-20 minutes until brown, basting several times with the reserved marinade; alternatively grill them under a hot grill for 20 minutes, turning occasionally and basting several times.

Serve the ribs whole or cut them into 6.5cm/2½in pieces using a meat cleaver.

>><<

A Ploughman's Lunch

Ploughing was hard, physical work, and the farm labourers spent the whole, sometimes cold and wet, day in the fields. For these ploughmen, mustard was an invaluable part of their lunch-on-the-job as it provided them with inner warmth.

PORK TENDERLOIN *glazed in* SUGAR *and* MUSTARD

Nothing is simpler to cook than traditional roast pork, but a coating of sweetened mustard cleverly elevates to culinary heights what might otherwise have been a commonplace dish. Serve it with a selection of vegetables such as Potato Gratin (page 92), Carrots Sautéed with Cumin and Coriander (page 92) or Golden Parsnip Mousse (page 98).

SERVES 4

1kg · 2lb pork loin or boneless	*2tbsp English mustard*
leg or shoulder	*30g · 1oz brown sugar*
vegetable oil for coating	*1½tsp clear honey*
crackling	*freshly ground black pepper*

Preheat the oven to 175°C/350°F/gas mark 4.

Brush the crackling with oil and sprinkle with salt.

In a bowl, combine the mustard, sugar and honey with salt and freshly ground black pepper to form a spreadable mixture. Make several incisions along the pork and rub the mixture all over it and into the incisions.

Place the pork in a roasting pan and bake in the pre-heated oven for about 2 hours until cooked. Cover the pork with foil for the last 30 minutes.

PEPPERED STEAK *with* MUSTARD SAUCE

Creamy mustard sauce, fortified with brandy, is an inspired and luxurious addition to the classic marriage of pepper and steak. Prepared in seconds, this is nonetheless a sophisticated dish that bursts with flavour.

Press the crushed peppercorns on to both sides of the steaks. Heat the oil in a large frying pan and add the steaks, in two batches if necessary. Cook for 2½ minutes each side for a rare steak, 4 minutes each side for medium, or 6 minutes each side for well done.

Remove the cooked steaks from the pan and keep warm. Add the mushrooms to the same pan, scraping up any bits of peppercorn, and fry for 4 minutes, stirring frequently. Pour in the cream and brandy, add the mustard and mix well, gently heating the cream through without boiling it.

Serve each steak with some sauce poured over the top.

SERVES 4

4tbsp mixed peppercorns,
   crushed

4 sirloin steaks

2tbsp olive oil

180g • 6oz button mushrooms,
   halved

6tbsp double cream

5tbsp brandy

2tbsp English or whole grain
   mustard

SPICY INDIAN LAMB

Marinated in a spicy paste for one to two days then roasted for several hours and served with a heavily spiced sauce, this is a delicious, if unusual, alternative for the Sunday leg of lamb. The tasty sauce is very versatile and can be used, without the added meat juices, with many other dishes. Chapatis (page 106)

SERVES 4

1.25-1.5kg • 2½-3lb leg of
  lamb, trimmed of fat
4tbsp vegetable oil
MARINADE
150ml • ¼pt white wine
2 cloves garlic
2.5cm • 1in piece fresh root
  ginger, peeled and roughly
  chopped
1 green chilli pepper, seeded
  and roughly chopped
1 onion, roughly chopped
2tsp yellow mustard powder
1tsp ground coriander
1tbsp mixed peppercorns,
  crushed
1tsp ground cumin
1tsp ground cinnamon
SAUCE
1tbsp vegetable oil

2 shallots, finely chopped
2tsp black mustard seeds
1 small green chilli pepper,
  seeded and finely
  chopped
2 cloves garlic, crushed
1cm • ½in piece fresh root
  ginger, peeled and thinly
  sliced
½tsp ground turmeric
½tsp ground cumin
½tsp ground coriander
1 x 200g • 7oz can chopped
  tomatoes
1tbsp tomato purée
150-250ml • 5-8fl oz white
  wine, according to taste
½ lime, juice only
2tbsp finely chopped fresh
  coriander

go well with this dish.

Place all the marinade ingredients in a food processor and purée until smooth. Using a sharp, pointed knife, make several incisions in both sides of the leg of lamb; this will assist the marinating process. Place the lamb in a large dish and pour the marinade over the lamb, rubbing it in. Cover with film and place in the refrigerator to marinate for 24-48 hours. Turn the lamb and baste it with the marinade at least twice a day.

Remove the lamb from the refrigerator an hour before cooking to allow it to reach room temperature. Preheat the oven to 200°C/400°F/gas mark 6.

Remove the lamb from the marinade, reserving the marinade. Heat the oil in a large roasting pan, place it on the hob and brown the lamb on all sides. Pour over the reserved marinade, cover the pan with a roasting lid or foil (making sure it does not come into contact with the meat) and roast in the oven for 1 hour. Reduce the temperature to 160°C/325°F/gas mark 3 and cook for a further 2 hours.

Take the lamb out of the oven and set aside to cool slightly. Then transfer the lamb to a warmed serving dish, reserving any meat juices. Strain the juices and skim off any fat: allow the juices to settle before spooning or pouring off the top layer of fat.

To make the sauce, heat the oil in a frying pan over medium heat and gently fry the shallots for 2-3 minutes until soft. Add the mustard seeds, chilli pepper, garlic and ginger and fry for a further 2 minutes. Stir in the turmeric, cumin and coriander. Then add the chopped tomatoes, tomato purée, white wine and any reserved meat juices. Cook over a low heat for few minutes until the sauce has reduced slightly. Stir in the lime juice and coriander leaves and heat through.

Either carve the lamb at the table and serve the sauce separately or carve it in the kitchen and spoon the sauce over the slices of meat.

MUSTARD MEDLEY

*ALL TRUE AFICIONADOS WILL FIND THIS A SURE-FIRE WAY OF WINNING CONVERTS TO THEIR
MUSTARD PASSION. ESSENTIALLY A SELECTION OF BOUGHT MUSTARDS LIVENED UP WITH ADDED INGREDIENTS AND
SERVED WITH COOKED MEATS, THIS IS A GREAT IDEA FOR AN INFORMAL SUPPER PARTY, BUFFET OR BARBECUE.*

For the main food you can mix spare ribs, chicken drum-sticks, sausages or burgers. Allow two of each per person. Grill the meats under a medium heat; the ribs and chicken drumsticks (with the skin kept on) should first be brushed with olive oil. (You could also try the rib recipe on page 72.) Grilled and roasted vegetables, too, can benefit from a mustard or two to bring out their flavours. Arrange the cooked meats and vegetables on large serving platters with the bowls of mustard scattered around.

All the mustards described here can be made on the day of use and require no curing to develop their flavours. However, for convenience they can also be prepared in advance, and will keep for a couple of weeks in the refrigerator. You can vary or augment the selection with your own choice of shop-bought mustards.

1. GARLIC MUSTARD
5tbsp French mustard
1 head garlic, roasted (see note right)
freshly ground black pepper
1 shallot, very finely chopped

2. OLIVE MUSTARD
5tbsp Dijon mustard
15 pitted black olives
  (about 30g • 1oz), finely chopped
1tbsp olive paste
1tbsp extra virgin olive oil

3. GINGER AND CORIANDER MUSTARD
5tbsp whole grain mustard
1cm • ½in piece fresh root ginger, very
  finely chopped
handful coriander leaves, finely chopped
1 clove garlic

4. DILL MUSTARD
5tbsp American mustard
1tbsp sour cream
2tbsp freshly chopped dilll
freshly ground black pepper

5. SUN-DRIED TOMATO MUSTARD
5tbsp Dijon mustard
45g • 1½oz sun-dried tomatoes in olive
  oil, drained and puréed
1tbsp finely chopped fresh tarragon
  leaves, or 2tsp dried tarragon

To make up the mustards, combine the ingredients in a small bowl. Note: To roast the garlic head for the garlic mustard, wrap the whole garlic in foil and roast in an oven at 200°C/400°F/gas mark 6 for 30 minutes. Remove from the oven, unwrap and carefully squeeze out the softened garlic from each clove and mix together with the other ingredients.

77

78

PAN-FRIED COD *with* CAPER *and* MUSTARD SAUCE

This simple-to-prepare dish bursts with flavour. The coarse grain mustard adds bite and helps thicken the sauce, while the black mustard seeds lend earthiness. Serve with wedges of freshly cut lime to squeeze over the fish.

SERVES 4

4 cod steaks or fillets	*2tsp black mustard seeds*
30g • 1oz plain flour, seasoned with salt and pepper	*1tbsp coarse grain mustard*
	2tbsp chopped fresh coriander
3tbsp olive oil	*4tbsp olive oil*
2tbsp capers (about 40)	*1 lime, juice only*
60g • 2oz pitted green olives, chopped	*freshly ground black pepper*

Dust the cod pieces with the seasoned flour. Heat the oil in a frying pan over a medium heat and shallow fry the fish for 5 minutes.

Meanwhile, mix together the remaining ingredients to make the sauce. Turn the fish over in the pan and pour the sauce over the fish. Continue to fry for a further 5 minutes, or until the fish is cooked through.

PASTA *with* ROASTED PEPPERS *and* WILD MUSHROOMS

Wild mushrooms add a distinctive rich flavour to this dish. If you cannot find any, you can use cultivated mushrooms, but the result will be slightly less intense. It is well worth the effort of removing the bitter skins from the peppers. The amount of mustard you include will depend on your personal taste. Add a little at a time, mixing well and tasting. Serve with a salad and an Italian Country Loaf (page 111).

SERVES 4

1 red sweet pepper	60g • 2oz wild mushrooms,
1 yellow sweet pepper	such as chanterelle or ceps,
250g • 8oz bow pasta (farfalle)	wiped clean and torn into
knob of butter	pieces
freshly ground black pepper	90g • 3oz chestnut mushrooms,
1tbsp olive oil	wiped clean and quartered
1 small onion, finely chopped	250ml • 8fl oz single cream
	2-4tsp whole grain mustard
	salt

Preheat the grill to hot and place the peppers under it to blacken the skins. Turn them regularly to ensure all the skin is blackened. Carefully remove them from the grill, place them in a plastic bag and seal. Leave for 5-10 minutes. Once the peppers have cooled sufficiently, remove the skins, deseed and slice.

Cook the pasta in plenty of boiling water. Drain, reserving 1 tablespoon of the cooking liquid. Transfer the pasta to a warmed serving dish, adding a large knob of butter and plenty of freshly ground black pepper. Keep warm.

Heat the oil over a medium heat and add the onion. Fry gently for 5 minutes until soft. Add the peppers and cook for a further minute. Add the mushrooms and mix well with the peppers and onions. Cook gently, covered, for 4 minutes. Pour in the cream, stir in the mustard and salt to taste, adding plenty of black pepper. Cook for a further minute to allow the cream to heat through.

Pour the sauce over the pasta, adding a little of the reserved cooking liquid if the pasta has become too dry.

LEMON *and* MUSTARD MACKEREL

Mustard, especially the wholegrain variety, seems to have a special affinity with mackerel and this recipe uses plenty of it. Tie string around each fish to keep it closed and the stuffing in place during cooking. You can use any kind of string, the more rustic looking the better for a "peasant" effect, but make sure it is natural fibre and not plastic. Serve the fish with the string in place and provide scissors for snipping.

SERVES 4

2tbsp wholegrain mustard	*2tbsp capers (about 40)*
2tsp hot pepper sauce	*90g • 3oz pitted black olives,*
4 whole mackerel or trout,	*chopped*
gutted and deheaded	*1tbsp chopped fresh sage, or*
1 lemon, grated rind and 2tbsp	*1tsp dried sage*
juice only	*salt and freshly ground black*
60g • 2oz fresh breadcrumbs	*pepper*

Preheat the oven to 200°C/400°F/gas mark 6.

Mix the wholegrain mustard with the hot pepper sauce. Wash the fish and pat dry. Open the fish out flat, flesh side down, and press your fingers hard down along the backbone to release it. Turn the fish over and carefully remove the backbone. Spread the mustard mixture over the flesh.

Combine the remaining ingredients in a bowl to make a stuffing. Divide the stuffing into four parts and spread over the fish. Close up the fish and tie each one with string. Place on a greased baking tray and bake in the oven for 20 minutes, or until the fish is cooked through.

HONEY-MUSTARD SAUSAGES

The sweet, spicy sauce in this dish livens up what otherwise might be very ordinary fare. A neighbour suggested slitting the sausages because he wanted to get more of the tangy sauce on to the sausages when eating them. Mashed sweet potato would make an excellent accompaniment.

SERVES 4

2tbsp honey	*4tbsp soy sauce*
2tbsp English mustard	*12 sausages*

Mix the English mustard, honey and soy sauce together in a bowl.

Prick each sausage and cook either by frying or grilling. When the sausages are three-quarters cooked, remove them and carefully slit them down one side leaving 1cm/½in uncut at each end. Spoon 1-2 teaspoons of the honey and mustard sauce into each sausage and finish cooking them.

Meanwhile, warm the remaining honey and mustard sauce over a low heat. Remove the cooked sausages carefully without squeezing out any sauce and serve with the heated sauce.

Hot and Sweet

When honey is combined with mustard, such as in making barbecue sauces, marinades and bastes, it adds a subtle sweetness that rounds off the hot flavour, giving it a new dimension. But the honey must be used judiciously so that it does not overpower the taste of the mustard.

MEDITERRANEAN PRAWN PILAF

The inclusion of mustard in a Mediterranean dish is unusual but here it adds a new dimension to a traditional recipe. The mustard flavour itself is very subtle, influencing the overall taste. Adding another teaspoon of mustard at the last stage of preparation will give more bite to the dish.

SERVES 4

2tbsp olive oil	1tbsp chopped fresh oregano, or
2 cloves garlic, crushed	1tsp dried oregano
1 onion, sliced	125g • 4oz crumbled feta cheese
2-3tsp coarse grain mustard	60g • 2oz pitted black olives,
250g • 8oz long-grain	roughly chopped
rice	1tbsp chopped fresh parsley, or
200g • 7oz tomatoes, chopped	1tsp dried parsley
250g • 8oz shelled cooked	salt and freshly ground black
prawns	pepper

Heat the oil in a large saucepan and gently fry the garlic and onion for 3 minutes. Stir in 2 teaspoons of the mustard, add the rice and cook for 1 minute more. Add the tomatoes with 350ml/12fl oz of water, bring to the boil then reduce the heat to low and simmer, covered, for 10 minutes without stirring.

Add the prawns and oregano and cook for a further 5 minutes, or until the rice is tender, adding additional water if the rice becomes too dry.

Stir in the feta cheese, chopped olives and parsley. Season, adding 1 extra teaspoon of mustard if you like. Remove from the heat and leave for 5 minutes before serving to allow the cheese to melt slightly.

RABBIT *with* MARJORAM *and* MUSTARD

Rabbit cooked with mustard is a classic French dish. The amount of mustard used here is deliberately imprecise, leaving the final decision to personal taste. The butcher will joint the rabbit for you if you ask. This recipe works equally well with chicken (use four chicken breasts or eight small pieces) and makes a great dinner party dish.

81

SERVES 4

30g • 1oz flour for dusting	4 rashers rindless bacon,
salt and freshly ground black	roughly chopped
pepper	600ml • 1pt chicken stock
1 rabbit (about 1kg • 2lb),	300ml • ½pt dry white wine
divided into 8 portions	handful fresh marjoram leaves
3tbsp vegetable oil	1tbsp arrowroot
4 small onions or medium	7tbsp double cream
shallots, quartered	1½-2tbsp Dijon mustard

Season the flour with salt and pepper and dust each portion of rabbit with it. Heat the vegetable oil in a large casserole (with a lid) over a medium heat and gently fry the onion or shallot quarters for 4-5 minutes. Remove the onions from the casserole with a slotted spoon and set aside.

Add the rabbit pieces and chopped bacon to the casserole and brown on all sides. Return the onions, pour in the chicken stock and white wine and add the marjoram leaves. Simmer with the lid on for about 1-1½ hours until the rabbit is tender. Remove the rabbit pieces to a heated serving dish and keep warm.

Mix the arrowroot with 1 tablespoon of water and add to the rabbit cooking juices. Increase the heat and boil the juices for about 5 minutes to reduce by about a quarter. Reduce the heat, stir in the cream and Dijon mustard and season. Cook for a further 1 minute until the cream is heated through. Pour over the rabbit portions and serve.

TRADITIONAL ROAST CHICKEN *with* CHESTNUT STUFFING *and* GRAPE GRAVY

Mustard adds an extra dimension to the chestnut stuffing of this perennial old favourite, a theme that is carried over into the accompanying gravy.

SERVES 4

30g • 1oz butter
1 small onion, finely chopped
1 stick celery, finely chopped
60g • 2oz fresh breadcrumbs
60g • 2oz cooked or canned
   chestnuts, roughly chopped
2tsp mustard powder
1tbsp finely chopped fresh
   parsley, or 1tsp dried
   parsley

900ml • 1½pt chicken or
   vegetable stock
1 chicken (about 1.60-1.80kg •
   3½-4lb)
1tsp ground arrowroot
150ml • 5fl oz single cream
1tbsp wholegrain mustard
180g • 6oz white grapes,
   halved and seeded
salt and freshly ground black
   pepper

Preheat the oven to 190°C/375°F/gas mark 5.

Melt the butter in a saucepan over a medium heat. Add the chopped onion and celery and cook for 4-5 minutes until soft. Add the breadcrumbs, chestnuts, mustard powder, parsley and sufficient stock to moisten the mixture.

Stuff the chicken with half the mixture. Make balls with the remaining stuffing and set aside. Place the chicken in a roasting pan, pour 450ml/¾pt of stock around it and season. Bake the stuffed chicken in the preheated oven for about 1½ hours, until the juices run clear. Baste occasionally during cooking with the stock and juices. Add the stuffing balls to the pan for the final 20 minutes. Remove the cooked chicken and the stuffing balls to a warm serving dish and allow to rest.

Meanwhile skim the fat from the cooking juices and place the roasting pan over a high heat. Add the arrowroot and boil rapidly until thickened and slightly reduced, adding additional stock if there is insufficient liquid. Pour in the cream, add the mustard and bring back to the boil. Finally, add the grapes, season and gently heat through.

Serve the roast chicken accompanied by the stuffing balls and grape gravy.

Love Potions

Ever since there was love there have been love potions, with the most successful use of herbal aphrodisiacs portrayed in Shakespeare's A Midsummer Night's Dream. And, if you are inclined to believe in the power of natural remedies, then a love potion might still lend a helping hand. The mustard plant is a crucial ingredient: used throughout history as a symbol of fertility because of its ability to reproduce on such a prodigious scale, it is also prized for its ability to withstand even the most unfriendly conditions (mustard seeds can lie dormant in the soil for up to a hundred years and still remain viable).

Both of these qualities make it invaluable in a love potion. Try this potent concoction of herbs and see how the recipient of your passion reacts .

A PINCH OF FENNEL SEEDS (NOT ONLY AN APHRODISIAC BUT ALSO SYMBOLIC OF FLATTERY)

THREE MUSTARD FLOWERS

A SPRIG OF ROSEMARY (AN ANCIENT WEDDING SYMBOL, AND SIGNIFIER OF REMEMBRANCE)

A SPRIG OF LAVENDER (A TRADITIONAL TOKEN OF AFFECTION)

A FOUR-LEAFED CLOVER (A TOKEN FOR LUCK)

Lightly crush the fennel seeds in a pestle and mortar and then infuse them in boiling water with the other ingredients for 10 to 15 minutes. Strain the mixture and discard the herbs. The remaining liquid should then be drunk as a tea.

83

Mustards to Make

THE FOLLOWING RECIPES SHOW YOU HOW TO MAKE YOUR OWN DELICIOUS MUSTARDS. USE THEM TO ACCOMPANY MEATS AND CHEESES OR IN SAUCES, DRESSINGS, SOUPS AND STEWS.

Mustards are easy to mix up. Those featured here all use freshly ground seeds which require a few minutes soaking to release the flavours. Once mixed they can be spooned into jars, small bowls, small ramekins or pots, then tightly covered and stored in the refrigerator for at least two to three weeks to allow their flavours to develop. They are then ready to use. All the mustards given here should keep in a cool, dark place for up to one year, but if they are continually re-opened and closed, they will begin to lose their pungency and taste blander after six months. If a stored mustard becomes too thick, add a few drops of water.

Mustard seeds can be ground using a pestle and mortar or, if you have one, a coffee grinder that you keep especially for spices. The seeds are finely ground to release all the flavour, except where a coarse or chunky texture is required.
The same method can be used for all these mustards:
Place the ground mustard seeds in a bowl, add sufficient water to moisten them and leave for 10 minutes.

Place the soaked ground mustard seeds in a food processor with the remaining ingredients and blend thoroughly.

Spoon the mustard into a jar, small ramekins or pots, cover tightly, and leave for at least 2 weeks in the refrigerator before opening.

HOT CHILLI MUSTARD
The hot chilli flavour of this mustard is not apparent at first, but then it hits you in the back of the throat with a real wham. It is great with hot dogs, burgers, steaks and strong, mature cheeses. Try rubbing some into the skin of chicken breasts before grilling to give an extra kick. For smooth blending, add the olive oil with the blender in motion.

1tbsp yellow mustard seeds, finely ground
1tbsp brown mustard seeds, finely ground
3 small dried red chilli peppers, very finely chopped
1tbsp mustard powder
1tsp salt
1tbsp sugar
3tbsp red wine vinegar
2tbsp olive oil

PINEAPPLE AND CHILLI MUSTARD

A fruity, fairly cool mustard, this is excellent for those who like the taste of mustard but cannot take the heat. It is well suited to fish, duck and steak. Add a spoonful of mayonnaise or sour cream and you have a great party dip. If the mixture is too thick, add a tablespoon of the reserved pineapple juice.

3tbsp mustard powder
1tsp chilli powder
125g • 4oz roughly chopped pineapple, fresh or canned, drained with 1tbsp juice reserved if canned
1tbsp sherry
1tsp salt
1tsp dried oregano
1tsp dried thyme

CRUNCHY CRITUS MUSTARD

When grinding the seeds for this recipe, do so for a few seconds only. The coarsely ground seeds combined with the zest of the fruits will give the mustard a lovely crunchy texture. Use it with vegetables, fish and pork, or in marinades and dressings. The mustard seeds are left to stand in citrus juice for one week to allow them to absorb more of the flavours.

2tbsp yellow mustard seeds, coarsely ground
2tbsp brown mustard seeds, coarsely ground
1 lemon; zest and juice only
1 lime; zest and juice only
2tbsp soft brown sugar

HORSERADISH MUSTARD

If you like your mustard really hot, this is the one for you. It makes a fantastic accompaniment to sausages and mature cheeses as well as – naturally – traditional roast beef.

2tbsp horseradish sauce
4tbsp mustard powder
2tsp sugar
1tsp salt
4tbsp olive oil

Place all the ingredients in a food processor with 2 tablespoons of water and blend thoroughly.

Spoon the mustard into small ramekins or pots and cover tightly. It will be ready to use in 2 weeks.

GREEN HERB MUSTARD
This is a great all-round mustard with a fair amount of heat. Try stirring it into rice dishes or soups just before serving to give extra flavour.

2tbsp yellow mustard seeds, finely ground
2tbsp brown mustard seeds, finely ground
1tbsp fresh parsley, or 2tsp dried parsley
1tbsp fresh thyme, or 2tsp dried thyme
1tbsp fresh oregano, or 2tsp dried oregano
1 clove garlic, roughly chopped
4tbsp white wine vinegar
2tbsp olive oil
1tsp salt
freshly ground black pepper

CHERRY MUSTARD
A perfect accompaniment to pork, smoked meats and duck. If fresh cherries are unavailable, use canned or frozen ones. Although most canned cherries are sweetened with syrup, they can still be used for this summery mustard.

2tbsp yellow mustard seeds, finely ground
2tsp mustard powder
2tbsp raspberry wine vinegar
10 cherries, fresh, canned or frozen, pitted
*   and roughly chopped*
1tsp freshly ground black pepper
1tsp salt
1tbsp sherry

THAI-STYLE MUSTARD
The refreshing, limey flavour of this mustard makes it a useful sandwich spread. As a traditional mustard, it goes well with fish and chicken.

2tbsp brown mustard seeds, finely ground
4tbsp fresh coriander
2tbsp olive oil
1tbsp mustard powder
1tbsp light brown sugar
1 lime, juice only
2tsp finely chopped lemon grass, or 1tsp
*   dried lemon grass*
2tsp chopped fresh ginger root

TARRAGON MUSTARD

This is a very hot sweet mustard. If it appears too thick, add an additional tablespoon of tarragon vinegar. The mustard marries perfectly with chicken; it also makes a good sandwich spread and can be used in vinaigrettes for dressing salads and vegetables.

4tbsp yellow mustard seeds, finely ground
4tbsp chopped fresh tarragon, stems removed, or 1tbsp dried tarragon
4tbsp tarragon vinegar
1tsp salt
2tbsp sugar
2tbsp mustard powder
1tbsp clear honey

HONEY MUSTARD

Good for keeping in the larder as a handy baste for meats and fish, this sweet mustard needs a minimum of three weeks for its flavours to develop. Used sparingly, it also makes a tasty sandwich spread.

2tbsp yellow mustard seeds, finely ground
2tbsp mustard powder
3tbsp clear honey
4tbsp white wine vinegar
1tbsp green peppercorns, crushed
1tbsp brown sugar

CHAMPAGNE MUSTARD

This is a great way of using up that last drop of champagne. Alternatively, open a bottle of champagne specially to make the mustard, then sit back and think up a suitable reason to celebrate and finish off the rest of the bottle. If you are feeling slightly less extravagant, you can substitute a white sparkling wine. The mustard should be mixed by hand to preserve the champagne bubbles. Serve with poultry, vegetables and cheeses.

3tbsp yellow mustard seeds, finely ground
2tbsp mustard powder
1½tbsp honey
1tsp salt
2tsp sugar
75ml • 3fl oz champagne or sparkling wine

CHAPTER FOUR

VEGETABLES

Many varieties of vegetables from across the world are now available throughout the year. No longer just an adjunct to a main course, they can be a meal in their own right. Try aromatic stuffed peppers or a crunchy stir-fry to remind yourself what good partners mustard and vegetables can be.

VEGETABLES

The Romans used mustard on many vegetable dishes, sprinkling coarse ground seeds on dishes of green beans or beetroot in oil and vinegar dressing: two ideas which we can copy today. Cooked beetroot are delicious peeled and dressed while still hot and then eaten before they are totally cold. Baby beetroot make a marvellous hot vegetable tossed in a butter, lemon juice and grainy mustard, while large beetroot baked in the oven are great with a sauce made from crème fraîche, mustard and a little horseradish to offset the sweetness.

Indian vegetables dishes, either gently or fiercely spiced, often use mustard seeds to great effect. Potato dishes in particular tend to include some of the whole seeds, usually the brown or black type. Fiery little vegetable samosas normally include mustard seed to help spice them and pulses such as lentils benefit enormously from a touch of mustard seed in any spice mixture added to them.

>>>>>>>> <<<<<<<<

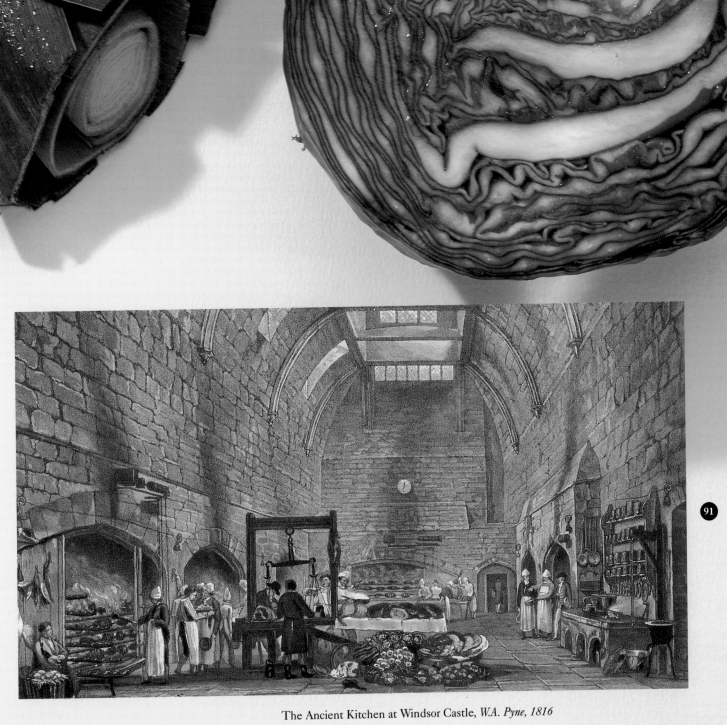

The Ancient Kitchen at Windsor Castle, *W.A. Pyne, 1816*

Colonel Mustard

The word Mustard has been immortalized in Colonel Mustard, the character in the famous boardgame Cluedo. Perhaps the originators of the game felt that "Mustard" was an appropriately fiery colour to represent this rather hot-tempered looking gentleman. Appropriately he is seen here in the kitchen.

POTATO GRATIN

Mustard, with a few other well chosen ingredients, really does something for potatoes. This dish is an ideal one to prepare if you are unsure about the time your guests will be arriving or when you will be sitting down to eat. Assemble the gratin, cook for one hour, then reduce the heat to low and allow the flavours to develop while you wait.

SERVES 4

3 potatoes (about 750g • 1½lb), skins on	1tbsp chopped fresh tarragon, or 2tsp dried tarragon
salt and freshly ground black pepper	150ml • ¼pt double cream
1½tbsp Dijon mustard	450ml • ¾pt chicken or vegetable stock

Preheat the oven to 190°C/375°F/gas mark 5.

Thinly slice the potatoes and layer up in a large, greased gratin dish, seasoning well between the layers.

Stir the Dijon mustard, chopped tarragon and double cream into the stock and pour over the potatoes. Cover with foil and bake in the oven for 1 hour. If necessary, you can keep the gratin warm on a low heat for a further couple of hours at this stage.

Remove the foil and bake for a further 25 minutes.

CARROTS *sautéed with* CUMIN *and* CORIANDER

This dish takes its inspiration from Indian cooking, where mustard seeds are often combined with spices such as cumin and coriander to flavour vegetable dishes. If you decide to cook this dish at a time of year when small, young carrots are abundant, use these instead of the large carrots called for and appreciate their heightened sweet flavour.

SERVES 4

3 large carrots (about 375g • 12oz)	1tsp black mustard seeds
30g • 1oz butter	1tsp cumin seeds
1tbsp vegetable oil	1tsp coriander seeds
	1tbsp soy sauce

Cut the carrots into three crossways and each of these pieces into thin strips.

In a sauté pan, heat the butter with the oil over a high heat then add the mustard, cumin and coriander seeds. Sauté for about 30 seconds until the seeds begin to pop. Add the carrots, turning them to coat them evenly with the butter and spices, and sauté for 1 minute. Add the soy sauce and continue to cook, covered, for a further 9 minutes until the carrots are just tender.

CRUNCHY VEGETABLE STIR-FRY

SERVES 4

1 tbsp vegetable oil
2tbsp black mustard seeds
1tsp cumin seeds
1 clove garlic, crushed
2.5cm • 1in piece fresh ginger root, peeled and cut into thin strips

10 radishes, sliced
100g • 3¼oz mangetouts, topped and tailed
10 baby sweetcorn
150g • 5oz fresh bean sprouts
4 spring onions, shredded

Heat the oil in a wok or heavy frying pan over a high heat. Add the mustard seeds and the cumin seeds and stir-fry until they begin to pop. (This will take only 30 seconds or so.) Add the garlic and ginger and stir-fry for a further 20 seconds. Add the radishes, mangetouts, baby sweetcorn and bean sprouts and stir-fry for 4 minutes. Finally, add the shredded spring onions and stir-fry for a further minute.

Stir-frying means cooking the food as quickly as possible to preserve flavour and goodness, which makes it an excellent way of preparing fresh vegetables. The mustard and cumin seeds should be stir-fried first to release their flavours early on. Serve this crunchy, colourful dish as part of a main meal or as a light lunch.

94

AROMATIC STUFFED PEPPERS

Using many of the spices traditionally found in Indian cuisine, these stuffed mini peppers are good as a vegetable accompaniment or buffet dish. If you fancy a sauce to go with them the sauce from Spicy Indian Lamb (page 75) goes particularly well.

SERVES 4

vegetable oil for frying
1tbsp black or brown mustard seeds
1 green chilli pepper, finely chopped
2.5cm • 1in piece fresh ginger root, grated
2 cloves garlic, crushed
105g • 3½oz Basmati or long grain rice
150ml • ¼pt white wine
150ml • ¼pt vegetable stock
1 large potato, diced
1tsp cumin seeds
1tsp ground coriander
1tsp ground paprika
8 small red sweet peppers
handful coriander leaves, roughly chopped

Preheat the oven to 190°C/375°F/gas mark 5.

Heat 1½ tablespoons of the vegetable oil in a large saucepan over a medium-high heat. Add the mustard seeds, chilli pepper, ginger and garlic and fry for 3 minutes until the vegetables are soft. Add the rice, mix well and cook for 2 minutes. Pour in the white wine and bring to the boil. Reduce the heat to low, pour in the stock and cook, covered, for 15 minutes. Lift the lid as little as possible during cooking, but if the rice appears too dry, add more stock.

Meanwhile, pour oil to about 2.5cm/1in deep into a frying pan and heat over a high heat. Add the diced potatoes and fry for about 12 minutes until golden on all sides. Remove from the pan using a slotted spoon and pour off all but 1 tablespoon of the oil. Heat the oil again until hot, add the cumin seeds and fry for 30 seconds. Add the ground coriander and paprika and fry for a further 30 seconds. Return the potatoes to the pan and coat in the spices, cooking for a further 1 minute. Remove from the heat.

To prepare the sweet peppers for stuffing, slice off the tops, reserving them, and remove the seeds.

When the rice is cooked, combine with the potatoes and add the coriander leaves. Fill each pepper with the mixture, replace the top as a lid and place on a baking tray. Bake in the oven for 20 minutes.

CORIANDER RÖSTI

96

Rösti is a national Swiss dish traditionally made with just potatoes and lots of butter. This mustard- and horseradish-flavoured variation adds new ingredients all nicely set off by plenty of fresh coriander. Serve it in wedges as a snack at any time of the day, as an accompaniment to a main meal, or wrap it in foil and take it on a picnic.

SERVES 4

4 potatoes (about 500g • 1lb), scrubbed	*1tbsp Dijon mustard*
2 parsnips (about 300g • 10oz), peeled	*3tbsp chopped fresh coriander*
1 apple, peeled	*salt and freshly ground black pepper*
2tsp horseradish sauce	*30g • 1oz butter*

Par-boil the potatoes in their skins for 10 minutes. Drain the cooked potatoes and rinse under cold water. Remove the skins and grate the flesh into a large bowl.

Grate the parsnips and apple into the same bowl and mix well. Add the horseradish, mustard, coriander and season to taste. Combine all the ingredients thoroughly.

Melt half of the butter in a non-stick frying pan, tip the rösti mixture into the pan and press it down with the back of a wooden spoon or spatula to form a flat cake. Cook over a medium heat for 10 minutes then carefully turn out the rösti on to a plate. Melt the remaining butter in the pan, return the rösti with the uncooked side down and cook for 5-10 minutes. The rösti should be golden brown on both sides.

ORIENTAL STUFFED CABBAGE LEAVES

Added whole to a dish, black mustard seeds impart an earthy savour which in this recipe mingles with the soy and hoisin sauces to give a strong, oriental taste. You can serve the stuffed leaves as the vegetable course of a main meal, or on their own as a starter.

SERVES 4

8 large green cabbage leaves	*8 shiitake mushrooms, soaked in hot water for 30 minutes if dried*
1tbsp olive oil	
2tbsp black mustard seeds	
2 cloves garlic, finely chopped	*4tbsp soy sauce*
1 red sweet pepper, finely diced	*4tbsp hoisin sauce*
8 baby sweetcorn, each chopped into 4 pieces	*4tbsp chopped fresh coriander*

Preheat the oven to 175°C/350°F/gas mark 4.

Blanch the cabbage leaves in boiling water for 5 minutes. Drain and refresh under cold water.

Heat the oil in a saucepan over a high heat, add the mustard seeds and allow to pop. Add the chopped garlic and stir-fry for around 30 seconds. Add the sweet pepper, shiitake mushrooms and baby sweetcorn and stir-fry for a further minute.

Pour in the soy and hoisin sauces. Cover and cook for 5 minutes, adding a little water if the mixture dries out. Remove from the heat and stir in the chopped coriander.

Divide the mixture between the 8 cabbage leaves, approximately 1 tablespoon per leaf, placing it in the middle of each leaf. Fold in the sides and end of each leaf to form parcels and place them, folded sides down, side by side in a greased ovenproof dish. Bake in the oven for 15 minutes.

Too Much Mustard

These posters, produced by the Mount Horeb Mustard Museum in Wisconsin, USA, demonstrate the vast number and variety of mustards produced internationally, and the challenge to mustard fans of trying all of them! Not only do the types of mustards vary, from wholegrain to smooth and runny, from hot to sweet. Mustard manufacturers take a very different approach to packaging, some opting for traditional Dijon and monastic earthenware pots, while others favour the more modern convenience of squeezy plastic tubes and sachets. It is interesting to note that some producers have reverted to using variations of the original Greek name for mustard, as in Senap and Sinappi Senap.

GOLDEN PARSNIP MOUSSE

Converting parsnips into a mousse is a perfect way of coaxing out all of their sweet flavour, while the addition of mustard, cream and paprika enriches it further. Depending on the size of your food processor, you may need to blend the parsnips with the apple in more than one batch.

SERVES 4

2 parsnips (about 300g • 10oz)	*salt and freshly ground black pepper*
1 apple	*2 size 3 eggs, lightly beaten*
2tsp ground paprika	*125ml • 4fl oz double cream, chilled*
1tbsp Dijon mustard	

Preheat the oven to 190°C/375°F/gas mark 5.

Peel and roughly chop the parsnips and apple then blend them together in a food processor. Add the paprika, mustard and seasoning and mix. Lightly beat the eggs and mix these into the mixture. Blend for a further 2 minutes to obtain a smoother mixture. Chill for 30 minutes.

Whip the chilled cream until it forms soft peaks and gently fold into the chilled parsnip mixture.

Grease a 900ml/1½pt oven-proof dish and pour in the parsnip mixture. Cover with a sheet of greased greaseproof paper and place in a roasting pan half to three-quarters filled with warm water. Bake in the oven for 30 minutes. Carefully remove the greaseproof paper and cook for a further 10 minutes to brown the top. Serve hot.

LEEKS *with* MUSTARD *and* CHEESE SAUCE

In this filling dish, the delicate flavour of the leeks is admirably set off by the piquancy of the mustard and the bite of good, full-flavoured Cheddar cheese. The perfect accompaniment is mashed or baked potato.

SERVES 4

4 large leeks (about 750g • 1½lb), trimmed and washed	*300ml • ½pt milk*
	1½tbsp coarse grain mustard
6 slices ham, cut in two	*125g • 4oz grated Cheddar cheese*
45g • 1½oz butter	*salt and freshly ground black pepper*
45g • 1½oz plain flour	

Preheat the oven to 175°C/350°F/gas mark 4.

Cut the leeks into 3 pieces each and par-boil them in boiling salted water for 3 minutes. Drain them.

Wrap a piece of ham round each leek and place them side by side in a greased ovenproof dish.

Melt the butter in a saucepan over high heat and stir in the flour. Reduce the heat to medium and cook for 30 seconds, stirring frequently. Pour in the milk, stirring well to prevent any lumps forming. Add the coarse grain mustard and three-quarters of the grated cheese and mix well.

Pour the cheese sauce over the leeks, sprinkle the remaining cheese on top and bake in the oven for 20 minutes.

This charming late nineteenth-century advertisement, produced by Keen's of England, depicts a scene from Shakespeare's As You Like It *in which Celia and Rosalind quiz the Fool, Touchstone.*

ROSALIND
Where learned you that oath, fool?

TOUCHSTONE
Of a certain knight that swore by his honour that they were good pancakes and swore by his honour that the mustard was naught: now I'll stand to it the pancakes were naught and the mustard was good, and yet was not the knight forsworn.

The clever use of selective quotation allows Keen's to suggest that no less a person than Shakespeare was an advocate of their product.

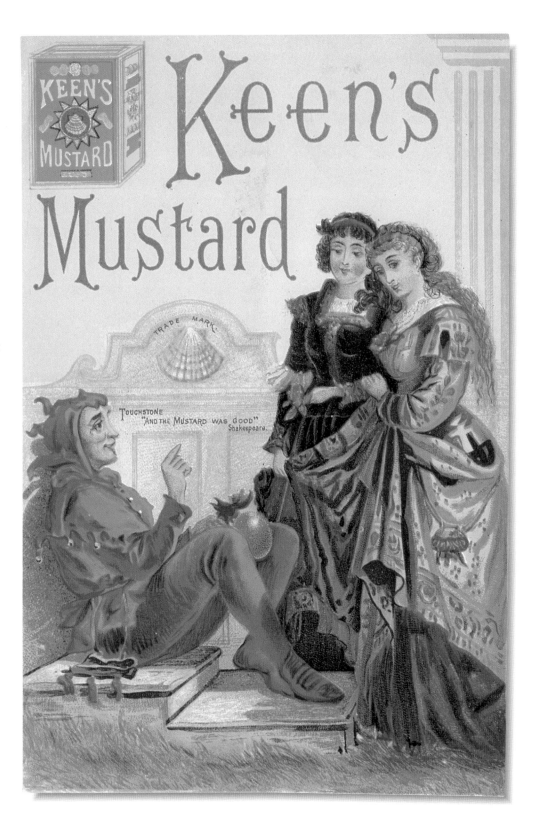

99

The Mustard Club

In the early twentieth century, the appeal of mustard was waning in Britain, so Colman's responded with a brilliant advertising campaign of a kind never seen before. They asked the S H Benson advertising agency to come up with a revolutionary new campaign, which turned out to be hugely successful.

The sides of London buses were used to carry the message "Has father joined The Mustard Club?" The club consisted of a group of fictitious people such as Miss Di Gester (the secretary), Lord Bacon of Cookham, Master Mustard, Lady Hearty and Signor Spaghetti, author of the famous song "O Mostardo Mio". The

RULES of the MUSTARD CLUB

1. Every member shall on all proper occasions eat Mustard to improve his appetite and strengthen his digestion.

2. Every member when physically exhausted or threatened with a cold, shall take refuge in a Mustard Bath.

3. Every member shall once at least during every meal make the secret sign of the Mustard Club by placing the mustard pot six inches from his neighbour's plate.

4. Every member who asks for a sandwich and finds that it contains no Mustard shall publicly refuse to eat same.

5. Every member shall see that the Mustard is freshly made, and no member shall tip a waiter who forgets to put Mustard on the table.

6. Each member shall instruct his children to "keep that schoolboy digestion" by forming the habit of eating Mustard.

The Password of the Mustard Club is "Pass the Mustard, please."

A bust of the main character of The Mustard Club, Baron de Beef, complete with monocle.

The six crucial rules of the club, displayed with an impressive heraldic device above them.

101

president was a monocled Baron de Beef and the password was, of course, "Pass the mustard, please", while the motto was "Mustard makyth Methuselahs". The heraldic shield of the club appeared on menus and restaurant cards independently of the campaign proper and helped boost the publicity for Colman's. Much of the success of the campaign was due to Dorothy L Sayers, who worked on it as a copywriter. She is better remembered, however, as the author of detective novels starring the aristocratic sleuth Lord Peter Wimsey. The campaign ran from 1926 to 1933 and spawned many spin-offs such as books, card games, badges and eight Mustard Club songs. Over 2,000 applications arrived when the offer of a badge was made, and extra jobs were created by Colman's to help meet the extra demand the campaign caused.

The main officers of The Mustard Club, from left to right: Miss Di Gester, Lord Bacon of Cookham, Master Mustard, the Baron de Beef, Signor Spaghetti and Lady Hearty.

An early full page advertisement from 1926 for The Mustard Club, in mock-serious style. Great efforts were made to make the whole thing appear credible, even if the words were clever nonsense.

CHAPTER FIVE

BREADS

*M*ustard is an ideal ingredient in savoury home-baked breads. Now that bread is once again becoming a central part of a healthier diet we are increasingly spoilt for choice as ever more delicious varieties become available.

BREADS

The sandwich gained its name in the eighteenth century. John Montague, the 4th Earl of Sandwich, was an inveterate gambler and rather than withdraw from the gaming tables to eat at the dining table, he preferred to have meat brought to him between slices of bread. This convenient snack became known as a sandwich. No doubt if the meat was beef or pork a generous dash of freshly made mustard was added. In fact, mustard has become a vital ingredient for both cold roast beef and ham sandwiches, not to mention cheese or even egg mayonnaise. Any food put between two slices of bread has to be well flavoured to hold its own. Imagine a toasted cheese and tomato sandwich: perfectly fine if a little dull. Now imagine it spread liberally with good grainy mustard – and it is transformed.

Mustard plays a crucial part in another bread-based dish – toasted cheese or Welsh rarebit. The mustard helps to cut across the richness of the cheese and provides a sharpness and edge which brings the whole thing amazingly to life. Mustard addicts will have their own preferences as to what type it should be; smooth, mild American or fiery British, or maybe even a grainy French one.

>>>>>>>><<<<<<<<

The Sower, *Jean-François Millet, 1850*

CHAPATIS *with* MUSTARD SEEDS

Mustards seeds are not normally baked into chapatis (flat, unleavened Indian bread) but here they add a slight crunch. If you cannot find chapati flour, a very fine-textured, low-gluten flour also known as ata flour, you can use equal quantities of plain and wholemeal flours instead. The chapatis can be served with a multitude of Indian dishes; try them with Spicy Indian Lamb (page 75).

MAKES 8

375g • 12oz chapati flour, or 180g • 6oz each of plain and wholemeal flour plus extra for dusting	*½tsp sugar*
	5tbsp vegetable oil
	2tbsp black mustard seeds
pinch salt	*45g • 1½oz butter, melted*

Combine the flour, a good pinch of salt and the sugar in a large bowl. Add half of the vegetable oil and rub into the flour with your fingertips. Gradually add 185ml/6½fl oz warm water, gathering the mixture together, until a soft dough is formed. Add the remaining oil and the mustard seeds and knead for about 2 minutes. Transfer the dough to a floured work surface and knead for a further 5-8 minutes. The dough should stop sticking to the work surface and become soft and pliable. Shape the dough into a ball, place it in a clean bowl, cover with a damp cloth and leave for 30 minutes.

Knead the dough for a further minute and divide the mixture into 8 portions. Work on one portion at a time, always keeping the others covered. Roll each portion into a ball then flatten it with the palm of your hand.

When all portions have been rolled and flattened, preheat a heavy-based frying pan or griddle over a high heat. Using a rolling pin, roll a flattened portion into a 20cm/8in disc, place it immediately in the frying pan and start rolling the next. Cook each chapati for 2 minutes on the first side, turn it over with a spatula and cook the second side for 2-3 minutes or until black spots start to appear. Turn the chapati over again and cook until black spots appear on this side, too.

Line a serving dish with absorbent kitchen paper and pile up the chapatis, brushing each one with melted butter as you work. The absorbent paper will prevent the chapatis going soggy.

ONION *and* ROSEMARY FOCACCIA

Focaccia is a deliciously moist Italian loaf made with olive oil. Wedges of this subtly flavoured version make a welcome addition to any meal, whether served hot or cold. Cut into thick slices, it can make a splendid ham sandwich, especially when spread with a herb mustard (page 86).

SERVES 4

500g • 1lb strong white flour	*5tbsp olive oil*
½tsp active dried yeast	*2tsp black mustard seeds*
1tsp salt	*30g • 1oz butter*
3tbsp roughly chopped fresh rosemary	*2 red onions, sliced*
	1tbsp rock salt

Combine the flour, yeast and salt in a large mixing bowl. Heat 300ml/½pt water until hand hot and pour into the mixing bowl with 2 tablespoons of the oil, 1 tablespoon of the rosemary and all the mustard seeds. Mix until the mixture has a dough-like consistency.

Knead the dough on a floured surface for 10-15 minutes. Place on a floured board or in a floured bowl, cover and leave in a warm place (average room temperature will do) for about an hour until it has doubled in size.

Roll out the dough to a 25cm/10in diameter round and place on a greased baking tray. Leave to rise for a further hour. Preheat the oven to 230°C/450°F/gas mark 8.

Heat 1 tablespoon of the oil with the butter in a saucepan. Add the sliced onions and cook gently for 20 minutes, stirring occasionally to ensure the onions remain well coated.

Spoon the onions over the risen dough to cover it. Pour over the remaining 2 tablespoons of oil and scatter over the remaining rosemary with the rock salt. Bake in the oven for 15–20 minutes until golden brown.

FIERY PEPPERONI PIZZA

Mustard, hot pepper sauce and pepperoni combine to make this pizza hot stuff. The topping also uses passata, a smooth sauce of sieved chopped tomatoes available in most supermarkets. This recipe makes one large thin and crispy pizza; if you prefer thick-crust pizzas, roll out the dough to 20cm/8in diameter rounds and increase the baking time to about 30–35 minutes.

SERVES 4

1tsp active dried yeast
300g • 10oz plain flour
1tbsp olive oil
TOPPING
125ml • 4floz passata

1tbsp yellow mustard powder
2tsp hot pepper sauce
250g • 8oz Italian mozzarella
   cheese, sliced
20 slices pepperoni sausage

To make the pizza dough, sieve the yeast with the plain flour into a large bowl. Add 150ml/¼pt lukewarm water and mix well. Cover and set aside for 30 minutes.

Add the olive oil and knead into a soft dough. Place on a floured work surface and knead for about 10 minutes. Return the dough to a clean bowl, cover and leave in a warm place (average room temperature will do) for 2 hours, or until it has doubled in volume. Preheat the oven to 200°C/400°F/gas mark 6.

Turn the dough on to a floured work surface and knead for 1 minute. Roll out to make a 30cm/12in diameter round. Carefully transfer the pizza base to a greased baking tray.

For the topping, mix the passata, English mustard and hot pepper sauce together and spread over the pizza base. Arrange the mozzarella slices and pepperoni sausage on top. Bake in the oven for 20–25 minutes, until the cheese is melted and the crust is golden.

>>>>>>>> <<<<<<<<

FRESH HERB *and* MUSTARD SCONES

The aroma of freshly baked scones heavy with warmed herbs and tangy mustard is nothing short of irresistible. Perfect for serving with morning coffee or afternoon tea, these savoury snacks will quickly vanish. They can also be filled with cheese or ham and taken on a picnic.

MAKES ABOUT 15

250g • 8oz plain flour
1tbsp baking powder
2tsp mustard powder
1tsp salt
45g • 1½oz butter, cut into
* small pieces*
1tsp sugar

1tbsp finely chopped fresh
* herbs, such as parsley,*
* thyme or oregano, or 2tsp*
* dried herbs*
1 shallot, finely chopped
freshly ground black pepper
175ml • 6fl oz milk

Preheat the oven to 230°C/450°F/gas mark 8.

Sift the flour, baking powder, mustard powder and salt into a large bowl. Rub the butter into the mixture using your fingertips. Add the sugar, herbs, shallot and black pepper and mix well. Pour in ¾ of the milk and mix in quickly. If the dough is too stiff, add the extra milk to soften it. Turn the dough on to a floured surface and knead 4 or 5 times with the heel of your hand. Shape the dough into a circle approximately 2cm/⅝in thick and using a pastry cutter cut into 4cm/1¼in rounds.

Place the rounds on a baking tray and bake in the oven for 10–15 minutes until golden brown. For soft scones, wrap them in a clean tea towel as soon as they are removed from the oven. For crusty scones, place them on a rack to cool.

>><<

High Flier

So many airline passengers consider that adding
a dash of mustard, like adding salt and pepper,
is vital to the enjoyment of their meals that mustard
producers supply very small tubes especially for
them, at considerable expense to themselves.

An Added Kick

As mixing mustard seed with wine or grape must is a traditional way of making mustard it is not surprising that mustards blend well with alcoholic drinks. An extensive range of mustards with the added dimension of any number of international wines and spirits is now available. Irish whiskey and Jack Daniels add an extra "kick", while sloe gin, made by steeping sloes, the fruit of the blackthorn, in gin sweetened with sugar, produces a uniquely mellow mustard. The addition of Guinness makes for a more full bodied, rounded variety, while Champagne adds a lighter, more delicate flavour.

ITALIAN COUNTRY LOAF *with* SAVOURY FILLING

The medley of wonderful tastes stuffed inside this freshly baked bread evoke sun-drenched Mediterranean hillsides. When the loaf is ready it should feel very hard and sound hollow when tapped. Leave it to stand for 10 minutes before slicing and eating it warm. It can also be eaten cold and is ideal for picnics.

MAKES 1 LOAF

1tbsp active dried yeast
1tbsp salt
500g • 1lb strong white flour
2tbsp olive oil
FILLING
2tbsp Dijon mustard
2tbsp roughly chopped mixed fresh herbs such as oregano,

parsley and thyme, or 1tbsp dried mixed herbs
20 black olives, pitted and roughly chopped
45g • 1½oz sun-dried tomatoes in olive oil, drained and roughly chopped
30g • 1oz ricotta cheese

First make the dough. Heat 275ml/9fl oz water until it is lukewarm. Pour half into a bowl, sprinkle the yeast over and leave to stand. Dissolve the salt in the remaining water. Sieve the flour into a bowl, make a well in the centre and pour the two liquids into it. Combine the mixture well with a metal spoon. Add the olive oil and mix again. When the ingredients are well combined, turn the dough out on to a floured surface and knead for about 10 minutes. Place the dough in a clean bowl, cover and leave in a warm place (average room temperature will do) for 1 hour to rise. Preheat the oven to 200°C/400°F/gas mark 6.

Turn the dough out on to a floured surface again and knead for a further 2 minutes. Divide the dough into two and roll out one half to a 25cm/10in diameter round.

For the filling, combine the Dijon mustard with the mixed herbs and spread evenly on the rolled-out dough leaving an uncovered 2.5cm/1in border all round. Sprinkle over the chopped olives, sun-dried tomatoes and ricotta cheese, again leaving the border uncovered.

Roll out the second half of the dough to the same size and place on top of the first. Moisten the edges of the two dough pieces and pinch together. Bake in the oven for 40 minutes, or until the loaf has risen and is golden.

PARMESAN *and* ALMOND MUFFINS

Parmesan cheese and almonds may seem an odd combination at first sight, but the almonds add crunch and the Parmesan sweetness. The generous helping of mustard develops the flavour of the muffins without being too strong itself. These light, little breads are quick and easy to make and are best served warm.

MAKES ABOUT 16 MUFFINS OR 32 MINI MUFFINS

125g • 4oz plain flour	*1 size 3 egg*
2tsp baking powder	*125ml • 4 fl oz milk*
salt and freshly ground black pepper	*40g • 1¼oz butter, melted*
	2tbsp English mustard
60g • 2oz freshly grated Parmesan cheese	*30g • 1oz flaked almonds*

Preheat the oven to 200°C/400°F/gas mark 6.

Sift the flour, baking powder and a pinch of salt into a large bowl. Add some pepper and the grated Parmesan cheese.

In another bowl, combine the egg, milk, melted butter and mustard. Pour the wet ingredients on to the dry ones and mix well.

Spoon the mixture into greased muffin or small bun tins and scatter the flaked almonds over. Bake in the oven for 20 minutes until golden brown.

111

All Boxed Up

The packaging and advertising of mustard has a colourful and well-attested history. For some reason this quite ordinary product, whether as a yellow powder or a ready-mixed paste, has brought out the best in advertising creativity. Now that mustard is often one product among many in an international food giant's portfolio, the quirky and stimulating packaging and posters have gone, probably for ever, but there still remain some wonderful examples of the old-fashioned approach to advertising.

Fine examples of early Keen's packaging, proving how successful the colour scheme of red and yellow was. It was not successful enough, however, to stop the company being swallowed up by its arch-rivals Colman's.

A marvellously robust John Bull strides across the world, delivering Colman's mustard to its furthest corners. The proud boast "By special appointment to the King" is clearly visible.

A typical piece of nineteenth-century American packaging, with an impressive head of the company's founder, J R Watkins. The design is more reminiscent of a medicine than a food package.

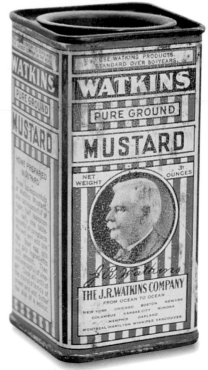

Patriotic emblems and symbols have been used to give this mustard plenty of credibility and Britishness. The company must have been a small one, and is not very well known.

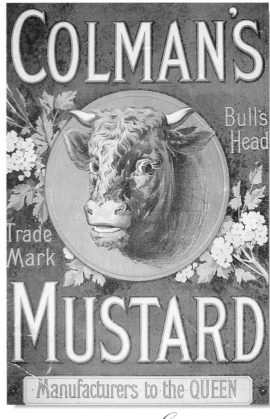

Many smaller mustard companies seemed to virtually copy the larger ones when it came to packaging. This design is reminiscent of both Keen's and Colman's, but the rather strange, Chinese-inspired "A" is intriguing.

Another company sensibly packaging their mustard in containers which could be used again. Mustard and some other food products are still sold in reusable containers in France today.

Colman's of Norwich used the bull's head symbol for many years in the early days of their advertising. In Britain, at least, mustard would always be linked with beef.

One of the mustard companies of Dijon (1816), draws on the town's history of the condiment to depict a medieval meal, with a toast, no doubt, to "Monsieur Moutarde".

113

Keen's, at one time probably Britain's best-known British mustard producer, commissioned these powerful graphics to ram home the name of the brand. The use of red and mustard yellow together is eye-catching and memorable.

A simple but striking design for Keen's powdered mustard. The shell symbol remains important and a dash of blue brings the red and yellow to life. Some people claim that the expression "as keen as mustard" comes from this company's name.

Amora mustards from France have often been packaged in reusable tumblers. Here are advertisements for two versions which hardly mention the mustard. One comes in a range of tempting colours inspired by the "aurora borealis" and the second has a 1950s interpretation of an African design.

A Savora advertisement from 1937, depicting all kinds of influences of the day, such as cinema and architecture. The artist's signature is prominent.

UNE SPÉCIALITÉ DE TYPE ANGLAIS

PLUS SUAVE QUE LA
MOUTARDE

PRICKLY
english savour

QUALITY
PRICKLY
QUALITÉ

BUVARD   BUVARD

A French mustard manufacturer making an "English" mustard seems on the face of it highly unusual. The name might have worked in France, but it is doubtful if it would ever have become popular in Britain.

A moon face – or is he a fiery, devilish mustard seed? These curious packaging labels from the beginning of this century (above and left) come from two of the many less well-known Dijon mustard makers

Je bonifie tout

La Préférée

MOUTARDE EXTRA
GARANTIE PURE
Stéphane PASQUIER
MOUTARDE TRUCHOT
USINE DE LA COLOMBIÈRE
à DIJON
CÔTE D'OR

L.PAGE & Cie

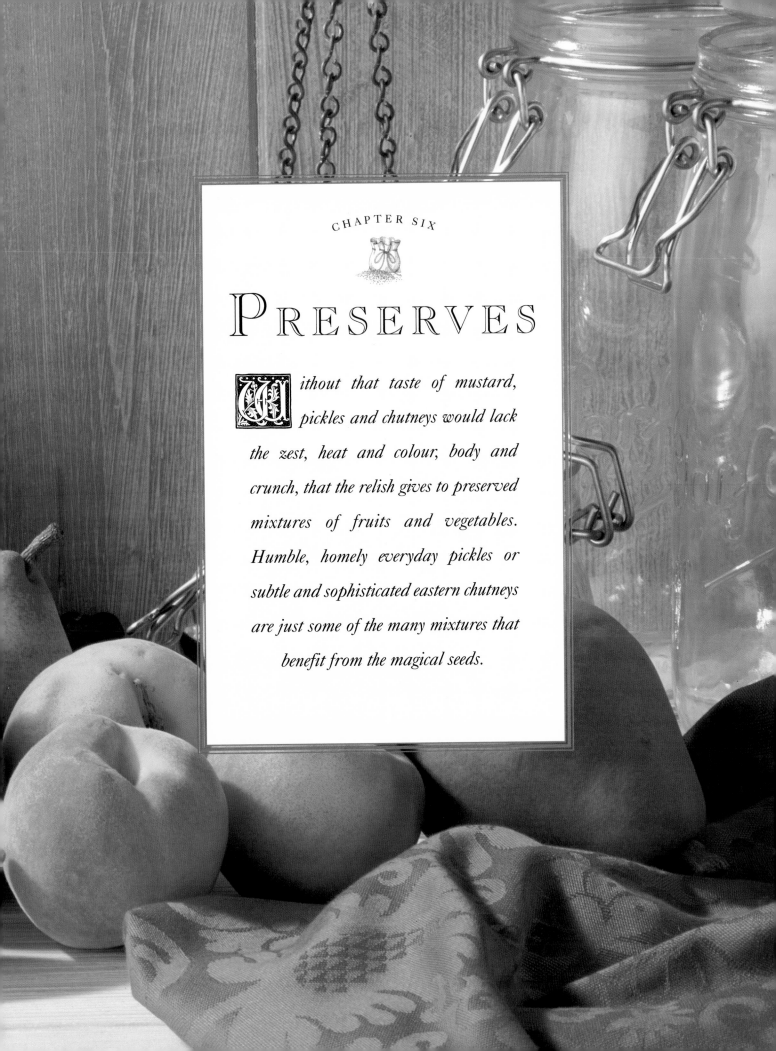

CHAPTER SIX

PRESERVES

Without that taste of mustard, pickles and chutneys would lack the zest, heat and colour, body and crunch, that the relish gives to preserved mixtures of fruits and vegetables. Humble, homely everyday pickles or subtle and sophisticated eastern chutneys are just some of the many mixtures that benefit from the magical seeds.

PRESERVES

Preserves were once an essential part of every well-stocked storecupboard, providing fruits and vegetables for lean winter months. Today they give colour and spice to the cook's palette and have become a really creative branch of cookery. Mustard is one of the most popular ingredients and plays an important role in many recipes for pickles, preserves and chutneys.

Generally, vegetables and fruits are pickled by individual type but mixtures are found too – such as those displayed in enormous jars in delicatessens with mixed vegetables packed inside with exquisite artistry. A spectacular Italian speciality is mostarda di frutta from Cremona, containing a variety of preserved fruits such as oranges, figs, plums, apricots, pears, cherries and slices of pumpkin and melon, flavoured with mustard oil in a bitingly hot sweet syrup. It is frequently eaten with the Italian mixed meat dish, bollito misto. Its origin dates from the days when sweet and sour flavours used together were commonplace.

>>>>>>>><<<<<<<<

Still life of fruit, *Cornelis Kruys, 1655*

SPICY TOMATO RELISH

A superb accompaniment for burgers and hot dogs, this relish will also wake up cold meats, enliven grilled chops or cheese and add surprise to sandwiches. If it is still not hot enough for some tastes, mix in a teaspoon of hot pepper sauce before serving. The relish is ready to eat after one week. Unopened, it will keep for up to three months.

MAKES ABOUT 1.75 LITRES/3PT

2.5kg • 5lb ripe tomatoes, cut into small dice
5 red onions (about 500g • 1lb), thinly sliced
1tbsp salt
1tbsp black mustard seeds
2tsp cumin seeds
4 long dried red chilli peppers
2tsp chilli powder
475ml • 16fl oz white wine vinegar
220g • 7oz sugar

Place the diced tomato and onion slices in a shallow dish and sprinkle with the salt. Leave overnight.

Using a pestle and mortar or coffee grinder, crush the mustard seeds, cumin seeds and chilli peppers.

Drain the tomatoes and onions and place them in a saucepan with the crushed spices, chilli powder, white wine vinegar and sugar. Bring to the boil, then simmer, covered, for 45 minutes, stirring frequently. Remove the lid and simmer for a further 15 minutes.

Spoon the relish into hot, sterilized jars, filling them completely. Cover with greaseproof paper discs and seal with screwtop lids or cellophane covers and rubber bands.

➤➤◄◄

The Earliest Mustard

Some of the earliest advice on preparing mustard is given in
De Re Rustica, *a treatise on farming and country life published in twelve volumes in the first century AD by Lucius Junius Moderatus, or Columella, a retired Roman legionary:*

"Clean the mustard seeds carefully. Sift it well and wash in cold water. After it is clean, soak it in cold water two hours. Stir it, squeeze it, and put it into a new, or very clean, mortar. Crush it with a pestle. When it is well ground, put it in the centre of the mortar, press and flatten it with the hand. Make furrows in the surface and put hot coals in them. Pour water with saltpetre over these. This will take the bitterness out of the seed and prevent it from moulding. Pour off the moisture completely. Pour strong white vinegar over the mustard, mix it thoroughly with the pestle, and force it through a sieve."

ITALIAN PRESERVED FRUITS

Fruit preserved in a mustard-flavoured syrup is a speciality of northern Italy. *Mostarda di frutta*, as it is known, is traditionally served with game and poultry. You can experiment with your own combinations of fresh and/or dried fruits; ones that immediately spring to mind are apricots, figs, pineapple, apples, pears, plums and nectarines. After bottling, store in the refrigerator where it will keep for several months. It is ready to be eaten after two weeks.

MAKES ABOUT 1 LITRE/1¾PT

400g • 13oz sugar
250ml • 8fl oz raspberry wine
    vinegar
2tsp mustard powder
2tsp yellow mustard seeds
1kg • 2lb mixed fresh and/or
    dried fruits cut into bite-
    sized pieces

Put half of the sugar into a saucepan with 250ml/8fl oz water and bring to the boil, stirring frequently and making sure the sugar dissolves. Add the fresh fruits you are using to the syrup and simmer for about 10 minutes until the fruits are tender.

Put the remaining sugar into another saucepan with the raspberry wine vinegar, the mustard powder and seeds. Bring to the boil and simmer for 5 minutes.

Allow both syrups to cool completely then mix them together and stir in the dried fruits.

Spoon the cooked fruits into hot, sterilized jars, ensuring that all the fruit is covered by the syrup. Cover with greaseproof paper discs and seal with screwtop lids or cellophane covers and rubber bands.

GRAPE AND GINGER CHUTNEY

Chutneys were devised in the Indian subcontinent to accompany curries and this strongly flavoured tangy, fruity version carries on the tradition. It is also excellent as a companion to fish, poultry and game. Store the chutney for at least four weeks before using. Unopened, it will keep for up to one year. If using white grapes store in a dark place to prevent discoloration.

MAKES ABOUT 350ML/12FL OZ

2tbsp vegetable oil
1tsp cayenne pepper
4tsp yellow mustard seeds
500g • 1lb white or black grapes

5cm • 2in piece fresh root ginger, peeled and grated
salt and freshly ground black pepper
250ml • 8fl oz white wine vinegar

Heat the oil in a saucepan, add the cayenne pepper with the mustard seeds and fry over a high heat for about 30 seconds.

Add the remaining ingredients, reduce the heat to low and cook, covered, for about 30 minutes. Remove the lid and simmer for a further 10-15 minutes until the mixture has the same consistency as thick chutney.

Pour into hot, sterilized jars, cover with greaseproof paper discs and seal with screwtop lids or cellophane covers and rubber bands

122

>> <<

Eliza the Tartar

The daughter of a Hastings brewer, Eliza Acton was the author of Modern Cookery *(1845) and* The English Bread Book *(1857). Both books were enormously popular and influential in England in the second half of the nineteenth century. Mrs Acton included recipes for both mild mustard, mixed with milk and very thin cream, and "an extremely pungent compound, which has many approvers" called Tartar Mustard, a mixture of Durham mustard, strong horseradish vinegar, cayenne or chilli vinegar and tarragon vinegar. Her advice was: "The great art of mixing mustard is to have it perfectly smooth, and of a proper consistency."*

MUSTARD PICKLE

Mustard pickles can be made with almost any combination of crisp vegetables, but matching cucumbers, small white onions, sweet peppers and cauliflower in varying proportions is a classic recipe. The result is often known as Piccalilli. You can serve this traditional pickle as part of a salad platter or as an antipasto. Keep it for at least three weeks before using. Unopened, it will last for up to three months.

MAKES ABOUT 1.75 LITRES/3PT

3 small cucumbers, roughly chopped into 2½cm • 1in cubes

500g • 1lb small white onions, halved

1 red sweet pepper, diced

1 small cauliflower, or ½ large one, broken into florets

2tbsp salt

600ml • 1pt malt vinegar

1½tsp mustard powder

2tsp yellow mustard seeds

1½tsp cornflour

1tsp ground turmeric

1tbsp, approximately, cider vinegar

2tbsp sugar

Put the cucumber, onions, sweet pepper and cauliflower in a bowl. Cover with water, add the salt and leave to soak for 8 hours.

Drain and rinse the vegetables under cold water to remove the salt, then put them into a saucepan. Pour in enough malt vinegar to almost cover the vegetables and bring to the boil.

Meanwhile, combine the mustard powder, yellow mustard seeds, cornflour and turmeric in a small saucepan and add approximately 1 tablespoon of cider vinegar, just enough to form a paste.

As soon as the vegetables come to the boil, add the paste and boil for 5 minutes. Add the sugar and boil for a further 3 minutes, or until the sugar has dissolved and the mixture has thickened.

Spoon the pickle into hot, sterilized jars, filling them completely. Cover with greaseproof paper discs and seal with screwtop lids or cellophane covers and rubber bands.

Banana *and* Raisin Chutney

A very sweet chutney, this partners strong cheeses, such as mature Cheddar, and cold meats particularly well. Keep the chutney for at least one month before using. Unopened, it will keep for up to two years.

MAKES ABOUT 1.25 LITRES/2PT

1 lemon	1tbsp yellow mustard seeds,
6 bananas (about 1kg • 2lb	crushed
including skins), peeled and	3tsp salt
sliced	1tsp ground nutmeg
250g • 8oz raisins	1.25 litres • 2pt malt vinegar
1tsp caraway seeds	500g • 1lb sugar

Remove the skin and pith from the lemon. Cut it into 1cm/½in slices then cut each slice into quarters.

Put the lemon slices into a saucepan with all the ingredients except the sugar, cover and bring to the boil. Add the sugar and stir to dissolve it. Simmer for 1½-2 hours, uncovered and stirring occasionally, until the mixture thickens to the consistency of a chutney. During the last half hour of cooking, check to make sure that the chutney does not become too dry and burn.

Pour the chutney into hot, sterilized jars, filling them completely. Cover with greaseproof paper discs and seal with screwtop lids or cellophane covers and rubber bands.

Fresh Corn Relish

Sweetcorn and mustard are a perfect relish marriage. Because the cooking time of a relish is less than that of a chutney, the vegetable pieces hold their shape and are identifiable in the finished preserve. This relish is ready to use after one week and will keep for up to three months.

MAKES ABOUT 600ML/1PT

75g • 2½oz sugar	500g • 1lb sweetcorn kernels,
1tsp salt	fresh or frozen
1tsp yellow mustard seeds	1 small green chilli pepper,
1tsp mustard powder	finely sliced
250ml • 8fl oz cider vinegar	1 onion, finely chopped
1 red sweet pepper, finely diced	

Put the sugar, salt, yellow mustard seeds and mustard powder into a saucepan, pour in the cider vinegar and 125ml/4floz of water and bring to the boil. Add all the remaining ingredients, bring back to the boil and simmer, covered, for 45 minutes, stirring frequently.

Remove the lid and simmer uncovered for a further 10 minutes. Increase the heat and boil the mixture rapidly for 5 minutes, or until the mixture is thick.

Spoon the relish into hot, sterilized jars, filling them completely. Cover with greaseproof paper discs and seal with screwtop lids or cellophane covers and rubber bands.

═══════ >><< ═══════

Shipwrecked

An eighteenth-century consignment of mustard and vinegar en route to Russia from France was lost when the ship carrying it was sunk off the Finnish Island of Jurasso. Salvaged in 1979, one of the original mustard pots is now exhibited at the Grey Poupon Mustard Shop in Dijon.

GENERAL INDEX

INDEX *of* RECIPES

127

ACKNOWLEDGEMENTS

Key: (a) above (b) below

Jean Pierre Pieughot/Image Bank 6, Bodleian Library 7, Mansell Collection 8, Food & Wine from France Ltd 8 (a), Roger-Viollet 8 (b), Harry Smith Horticultural Collection 10 (a), Mansell Collection 10 (b), Colman's of Norwich 11 (a), Mansell Collection 11 (b), Pictor 12–13, Harry Smith Horticultural Collection 14 (b), Dennis Davis/Ace 15, e.t. Archive 16 (a), Mansell Collection 16 (b), Roger-Viollet 17 (a & b), 18 (a), Bodleian Library 18 (b), Roger-Viollet 19 (a), Edmund Nagele/Ace 19 (b), Pictor 20, Edmund Nagele/Ace 21 (a), Colman's of Norwich 21 (b), Mansell Collection 22 (a & b), Colman's of Norwich 23 (a), Thierry Perrin/Rex Features 23 (b), Culpeper Ltd 24, e.t. Archive 25, Robert Opie 26 (b), 27, Bodleian Library 32 (a), Benelux Press/Ace 32 (b), Fotopic/Ace 33 (a), Roger-Viollet 33 (b), Gary Crallé/Image Bank 34 (a), Pictor 34 (b), Visual Arts Library 41, Peter Newark's American Pictures 50, Visual Arts Library 56, Thierry Perrin/Rex Features 52 (a), 53 (a & b), Colman's of Norwich 58 (a), Mount Horeb Mustard Museum 58 (b), Bridgeman Art Library 71, Harry Smith Horticultural Collection 83 (b), e.t. Archive 91, Bridgeman Art Library 105, 119, Mount Horeb Mustard Museum 97, Robert Opie 99, Colman's of Norwich 100–101, Robert Opie 112, Robert Opie 113 (a), Thierry Perrin/Rex Features 113 (b), Robert Opie 114 (a), Thierry Perrin/Rex Features 114.

All other photographs are the copyright of Quarto Publishing plc.

Quarto would also like to thank Chris Wilson at Colman's of Norwich for all his help and Elizabeth David Cookshop, The Piazza, Covent Garden, London EC2E 8RA for supplying equipment for photography.

Author's Acknowledgements (KH)

My thanks go to Tim, my chief taster, for tasting every recipe in the book, some several times. I would also like to thank Theresa and Ray for their endless trips to my kitchen and honest opinions. Thanks also to my sister Emma for helping out when deadlines loomed, and to all my other willing tasters, including Sue, Tony and Tina.